S0-DZC-302

THE AMERICAN
EMERGENCY

THE AMERICAN EMERGENCY

A Search for Spiritual Renewal
in an Age of Materialism

ROBERT BRIGGS

CELESTIAL ARTS
Berkeley, California

Copyright © 1989 by Robert Briggs. All rights reserved. No part of this book may be reproduced in any form, except for brief reviews, without the written permission of the publisher.

CELESTIAL ARTS
P.O. Box 7327
Berkeley, California 94707

Cover design by Ken Scott
Text design by Sal Glynn
Composition by Wilsted & Taylor, Oakland

Library of Congress Cataloging-in-Publication Data
Briggs, Robert, 1929–
    The American emergency: a search for spiritual renewal in an age
of materialism / Robert Briggs.
        p.   cm.
    Bibliography: p.
    Includes index.
    ISBN 0-89087-552-9. — ISBN 0-89087-546-4 (pbk.)
    1. United States—Civilization—1970– 2. United States—Reli-
gion—1960– 3. United States—Popular culture—History—20th
century. 4. Briggs, Robert, 1929– . I. Title.
    E169.12.B695   1989
    973.92—dc19   88-38176
                                                             CIP

Manufactured in the United States of America
First Printing, 1989
  1   2   3   4   5   6   7   8   9   0

CONTENTS

To William Weisjahn
1927–1969

PREFACE

What is the American emergency? Whenever the question is asked, it is interesting how few people deny one exists, though just as few are able to put a finger on exactly what it is. For me, the crisis is not only the threat to individual freedom and the clash between social extremes, but the result of insidious confusion brought about by change in the ultimate scientific paradigm that governs our lives. The problem has been identified by those who have recognized that the restrictions of determinism, so long so absolute, have been challenged by the freedom of uncertainty. The rapid deterioration of fixed values that resulted from this challenge has produced a growing mistrust of authority and led countless people to seek something more, something *other*. A powerful desire for change has resulted from the realization that established belief systems are not only obsolete, and no longer serve the general good, but threaten the future of fruitful existence. Dissatisfaction that in the 1950s was only vague uneasiness has become, in the 1980s, an intolerable infection that can no longer be ignored.

But what, exactly, can the concerned individual do? Faced with the freakish ruptures of technological achievements and caught in a malaise of mounting materialism, it has become obvious that to assure sane survival, concerned individuals must begin to assume far more responsibility for personal well-being and begin to utilize radical concepts of change. The agreeable assurance of the "expert" and accommodation to traditional ideals and graduated goals—once widely accepted guides to progress—have proven questionable and need to be critically reviewed.

The difficulty is that individual search for change not only requires the ability to recognize the difference between seeming change and *true* change, but also the vision to see beyond old borders, beyond the wavering line separating reality from mystery. Such vision is difficult to define, certainly impossible to determine scientifically; its origins reach back into endless spiritual planes of the soul. And before such recognitions can be achieved, the individual must learn to go within the self in order to gain a basic understanding of awareness and consciousness. The problem is that at this point change becomes complex, for individual variations obliterate neat general assumptions. What frustrates youth may serve those treading through the angst of aging. What inspires the obscure, baffles the well-endowed. What is right for the white, educated, middle-aged man may not apply to the younger black or Asian woman. Each human being must reassess current values and wisely rearrange ways and means by which whole new worlds can be experienced. Eventually, to transcend ordinary levels of awareness, it becomes necessary to *identify* considerations of the mind, body, spirit, and environment and *translate* these considerations into concerns with conduct, health, faith, and ecology; then through direct action—exercise, diet, meditation, and the alteration of lifestyle—*unify* all four in order to produce true change.

Today, unforunately, the importance of unification is rarely addressed. The parts may be brilliantly researched but, because of the tyranny of specialization, a whole picture is seldom drawn. As a consequence, unification is left up to the individual, who must begin the complex journey alone. This book is an account of one attempt to do just that.

When I began this work, I intended it to be a clear outline of considerations of consciousness and, above all, the problem of unification, having every reason to believe that a meaningful examination could be made. Most of my own life had been influenced by change and the peculiar freedom change produced; in addition, for more than ten years, I had been involved in the publication of works related to humanistic psychology, holistic medicine, spiritual renewal, and the "new physics." This experience, I felt, should have provided some advantage; unification, however, proved to be an enigma that defied solution. Eventually, with the help of others, I came to understand why unification was not easily addressed. It was not only that authorities in psychology, medicine, religion, and science were too confined to their own specialties, it was that any one discipline was incapable of addressing the whole problem. Unification proved to be an individual responsibility that could be secured only after an individual had returned to the self, mastered fundamentals of well-being, and realized that every facet of change affected freedom, even that freedom produced by social as well as scientific uncertainty. Recognition of social injustice was as important as attention to the dangers of physiological stress, and the struggle for sound ecology as vital as the need for spiritual enlightenment. After I discovered this, what was designed to be straightforward exposition became a personal collage arranged in a way that I hope will inspire others to reevaluate the constraints of traditional authority and fashion finer, more personal futures.

In this book I have tried to create a framework in which the current confusion over awareness and consciousness might be more carefully examined and understood. Drawing upon an odd but wide network of association, I have tried to capture—and order—the collective excitement that has become a foundation for human transformation and that has been heralded (somewhat inaccurately) as a New Age. While doing this I have come to see why events that seemed to have promised a New Age have, instead, delivered an Open Age—a split-action period in which defeat can bring victory and victory can occasionally lead to what Rupert Brooke saw as

> *Perplexed and viewless streams that bear*
> *Our hearts at random down the dark of life.*

The contradiction of a New Age is that what appears right can prove wrong; the advantage of an Open Age is that any event is incidental to those who have learned it is possible to go far beyond ordinary limits of accepted understanding. Yet in the end, whatever the comparisons or conclusions, only courageous intention provides a difference, only positive passion paves a way.

PART ONE

HANDMADE HISTORY

*Is it possible that the whole history of the world
has been misunderstood? . . .
Yes, it is possible.*

—*Rilke*

Looking back, it seems as if I always believed change would produce larger life. Without such faith I could never have dodged convention or endured a lifelong love affair with books, a romance that helped expose illusion and ultimately provided me with a livelihood. I was only six months old when the stock market crashed in 1929; that year Einstein published his Unified Field Theory and Thorstein Veblen died in the woods near Stanford University. In New York construction of the Empire State Building had begun, but before it was finished the Great Depression would split the national vision into sideshows spiced with piano music and scabbed with distress.

My parents were kind progressives who were never destitute but knew nothing of Thorstein Veblen. They were too frightened of the times, the unemployment, the hunger, the bloody strikes, and the gaunt faces outside the White House watching President Herbert Hoover who, in an attempt to restore confidence to the nation, ate his dinner in white tie and tails. By the time I was six years old, I loved to read and found endless inspiration in the rich seasons of the Middle West. Bicycling through the splendor of Hanscome Park and riding huge green streetcars past the shadows of screened porches, I mastered the geography of avenues and alleys by believing in the charm and drama of every block. Summers I spent stoned on the thunder of the Omaha stockyard, the second largest stockyard in the world at that time. From atop its twin wooden viaducts, I studied the vast system of pens and chutes knitted against the cavernous openings of the slaughterhouses, and spied on the shouting commission men who whipped and drove the terrified cattle. It was my introduction to fiction.

Growing up, I was always troubled by the endless budget of worry that seemed to level local lives; days and nights of ten-cent opera and mindless family matters inhibited by Irish Catholicism and passionate concern over Franklin Roosevelt's presidency. Because most of my people believed in politics and the drama of the mass, a gap developed between what I imagined life should be and what I experienced, especially after the atom bomb ended World War II. By then I yearned for greater magic and spiritual sustenance that would not be dissolved by parlor arguments or world conflict.

Encouraged by a tolerant mother and father, I haunted libraries and bookstores and read indiscriminately. To appease both sides of my Gemini division, I coveted the grand and the obscure with equal humility and with some confusion—once trading my father's leather-bound edition of Emerson's essays to my grandfather for a copy of *Oceanic Steamships*—just because of the illustrations. In such an American mix, confusion was undefined, but youth had an affinity with truancy and wonder that soon withered. Every year, as radio and billboard prophecy rose and fell with each new detergent, all kinds of otherness bloomed from bookshelves. Bacon glared at Shakespeare and De Maupassant was stoic about George Meredith and Henry James silently suffered the fact that Robert W. Service leaned against Edith Wharton. Eventually I discovered Conrad and Dostoyevski and, true to the times, stalked the tense jungles of Ernest Hemingway, revering his "grace under pressure." The voices of Hawthorne, Whitman, and Eliot marred this macho march, but literature was soon overshadowed by the painful fact that my family moved to New York City and I could get nowhere on a bicycle.

In New York I needed a car.

There was little appreciation of *seeing* then. Few people, save grim Freudians, speculated on how layers of the self could be peeled away to reveal the process of lives, and no one defined the dangers of conformity. At college I played football with psychotic zeal and prayed that the hundred-yard run and the roar of the crowd would carry me through liberal arts. Nothing of the kind happened, of course; and instead I was swept into the Cold War draft and ended up squatting inside filthy Korean bunkers, where Oh Henry! candy bars were stuck between sandbags. Because it was usually too dark to read, the only relief came from listening to shortwave baseball scores or the progress of truce talks at Panmunjom.

Out of the Army I went to New York City to finish my education at Columbia University, but the advantage of the GI Bill could not overcome years of academic incon-sistencies. The only peace I found was in cavernous Butler Library, where I interrupted days and nights of reading with casual attendance at random events and lectures. Semesters finally melted into a single afternoon when I abandoned a fashionable gray flannel suit in a rented room on 114th Street. No longer the promising young man who might use a college degree as insurance against unemployment (my father repeatedly advised that if nothing else worked out "you can always teach"), I announced I was leaving for Europe. It was the only removal I believed dramatic enough at the time, though it took a year to save the money necessary just to get out of Manhattan. This was a painful price to pay, for I quickly discovered I despised offices. When I finally did reach Paris, the winter was bitter. I stayed in a small Hotel Helvetia, but was too poor to wander very far, so, leaving more fortunate existentialists at the Flore and Deux Magots, I returned to New York.

In Greenwich Village I got a job at the Marboro Bookshop on 8th Street where, ignoring those who merely wanted out of the cold, I unpacked remainders, restocked shelves, waited on customers, and guarded against shoplifters. The scene was so fascinating I was never tempted to join tougher clerks who smirked at customers who asked for books by "Cam-moose." Late at night, walking through the moonlit streets of the Village, I stopped to drink dark beer at the White Horse Tavern or listen to jazz in half-empty basement clubs, where Negroes sat around small Formica tables with white women in dark corners, a long way from Omaha.

After four years of bohemia I left New York for San Francisco and, acting out a brief marriage and collection of short-story jobs, rode the crest of turbulent social change. In North Beach, intoxicated by the euphoria of the Beat Generation, I smoked Mahaba cigarettes, read poetry and listened to jazz, began a journal, and became involved with the Cloven Hoof, a Grant Avenue bookstore in which the idealism was notable and the cash flow inconspicuous. It proved to be the eye of a growing revolution. By 1957 the Beat Generation had lit the first fuse. Refusing to conform, consent, or consume, the Beats ignited smoldering brush-fires of social protest. Long before the successful folk singer or the bomb culture, long before the radical student, counterculture engineer, or Whole Earth visionary, the lonely Beat figure sketched formulas of resistance across suffocating swells of American materialism. In the Cloven Hoof, late-night faces, beginning to dissolve behind beards and long hair, discussed Sartre, Kierkegaard, and de Ropp's *Drugs and the Mind,* and rarely mispronounced *Camus.* But the Beat Generation was doomed. Distorted by the media and satirized by academic and cultural critics alike, the cool Beat insistence was discredited and finally evaporated in a psychedelic mushroom of political turmoil that fermented in the Haight-Ashbury and engulfed every university from Berkeley to Boston. The delicate Beat no and lonely kitchen introspection were swept away by an electrified radicalism that fried cool jazz and ignored the wonder of solitary introspection.

Tired of living on the edge and disenchanted with outside experience, I wandered into calmer neighborhoods. Disillusioned with drugs, rebellion, and alcoholic existentialism, I came to realize that many heroes were not heroes after all; recurring dreams of terrified cattle helped me see violence as an evil roughage that infected the century. By then part-time jobs could not support a search for change; they only induced a dreadful absence of wonder. Hemingway became a rusted relic who ended his own story by sucking on the shotgun that became as famous as his pen.

I made many attempts to establish alternatives; finally, in 1967, I secured a position as a sales representative for a large New York publisher. This was change. Every January and June, properly suited and groomed and lugging a briefcase full of fact sheets and order forms, I set out from San Francisco to sell the company's list in thirteen western states . . . carrying a half-dozen bestsellers and countless badsellers that would be shredded before the authors discovered they were obscure. It took only a couple of seasons to become confident about plotting appointments with chain store buyers and wholesalers, and less time to readapt to the world of bookselling. Between the green cash registers, fierce opinion was still modified by eccentricity and dedication. One of the finest-managed stores would not carry the work of Jack Kerouac, just as years before it had not carried Theodore Dreiser.

In those days thirty thousand new titles a year were offered to the nation. New lists were typically launched at elaborate New York sales conferences. Fall and spring catalogs were distributed to major accounts across the country, and these were followed by promotion, publicity, quotes, reviews, and public appearances by prominent authors. I soon realized that behind the scenes, publishing was actually a kind of cultural roulette played by tough professionals, and though I developed lasting respect for many individuals in the trade, other enigma had begun to sour my soul. I was nearly forty years old and had begun to measure life differently. It seemed to be leaking away, creating a hunger I could not satisfy. I was no longer thrilled by jetting between San Francisco and Seattle or Salt Lake City inside aluminum tubes filled with united aisles of agonized faces, and no longer enjoyed expense account restaurants, where carpeted restrooms were still marked Guys and Dolls, places where other publishing representatives drank because of the bad books they had to sell and the good books they could not.

These repetitions festered on the surface of my sanity until one night in the Denver airport, waiting for a delayed flight, I decided to do something about it. It was dawn when I finally soared out over the Rocky Mountains, and I landed in San Francisco determined to give myself other levels to deal with an inexorable *sameness* that seemed to be infecting every aspect of my life. This decision, and much more, revived my faith in change, which by then was little more than an odd condition impossible to explain to others who, caught in similar circumstances, could never be called upon to share another's burden. It often seemed as if some essential continuity had so unraveled that, for the dedicated observer, suicide and financial success seemed equally vulgar. Oddly enough, I believed change was still possible and more than ever was inspired to look for it. Such faith called for keen considerations; above all, it required risks. But after a depression, a world war, the Bomb, the holocaust—after the Cold War, marriage, fatherhood, divorce, and Watergate—any change was welcome.

Change came in the form of a partnership in a local San Francisco book company. Along with valuable publishing experience, this provided an opportunity to begin to examine early alternatives to traditional ideas of diet and life, but I needed more. I needed to act *into* something. I needed to find a way to go beyond what I had become. How to bring significant change to my life was still unclear, and where to begin was even more a mystery. I began to suspect that I needed to reappraise old, fixed habits and transcend the broad influence of accepted psychology, medicine, science, and religion. I needed to exhume the old patterns before hoping to transcend them. Serious contemplation warned that this could be confusing and would have to be pursued with great care if I were to avoid needless discouragement.

1972 was soon over.

I was still free of the responsibility of an immediate family, but sensible enough to know that this ensured nothing. Back in North Beach, I walked up Grant Avenue past the old location of the Cloven Hoof, where countless headshops and fox-and-flash boutiques had come and gone. As I crossed Green Street near the Savoy Tivoli, I noticed my reflection in glass storefronts and visualized a fractured progression of past times and places—the many moves I could have made and opportunities I could have exploited. But it was useless to think of all of that, so, following Green Street farther west, I decided to remain independent and play whatever chance came my way.

I had been in San Francisco more than fifteen years and was living in the Cow Hollow district, where I shared a two-family home owned by an elegant seventy-four-year-old woman who lived downstairs and offered sherry when I paid the rent, even if the payment was late. Upstairs a large off-white living room stretched across the front of the building and, anchored on each side by identical windows, a fluted fireplace divided the space in such a way as to provide ample room to conduct business and still entertain. A block away Union Street provided shops and restaurants, and a pleasant ten blocks north was the Marina Green, where I could walk on the edge of the bay and enjoy the Golden Gate Bridge or study the ruins of Alcatraz prison, which had been trashed by American Indians in the civil rights riots of the late 1960s.

The bookshelf was still the only shelter I could trust. Visual art had become eclectic and exclusive, films beguiled perception with size and sound, and music electrified discrimination. Only the book seemed permanent. Books were portable transportation, private exhibitions, hand museums, stages for idyll or rebellion against the unforgivable. Best of all, they could be more meticulously compared than most forms of expression. At any point an author's performance could be halted and calmly dissected; the quality of opinion and content could be mercilessly examined. The impression, voice, and character of the work could be isolated and analyzed on a variety of levels. Unfortunately, few appreciated the awesome process from which it emerged. The writing of a bad book could be as deceptively intoxicating as the writing of a good one could be torturous. Honest writers were tenacious vagrants who strung thousands of words into inviting tapestries, but their labors were piteously isolated. They could enjoy neither the physical relief of the painter or sculptor, nor the harmonic vibration of sound that sustained the musician. Whereas a painter might benefit from the study of a finished piece or a musician perform a neglected work, the writer drew little satisfaction from an unpublished manuscript. Until it was published, the written work was without blood or body. Only the poet suffered worse quarantine and faced the same submission before editors and agents who, in the contradictory quest for quality and commercial appeal, were often trapped between the painful extremes.

As another autumn began I decided to resign from the

local book company and begin a publishing association in which I could function as a literary agent and book packager. By drawing on a West Coast circle of freelance talent, I could devote unusual attention to projects I felt were good, or at least different. To a certain extent this was what happened, although hardly in ways I had imagined. Alone, in higher times, I had envisioned bold experiments—books with scented or mirrored pages, books with minute transistors buried in the spines that would play voice-over narrations or background music when certain passages were reached. I speculated about daring photographic novels, celibacy guides, and death manuals but, in the end, most of the dreams evaporated and the association worked terribly hard just to deliver finished manuscripts and to furnish authors with guidance not usually found in the publishing world.

One of the primary aims of the association was to find good fiction, but this goal proved elusive. Despite contemporary innovations and the powerful influence of new women writers, too many novels pandered to pop attitudes and the influence of films that magnified violence and sexual extremes in order to support cinematic virtuosity. This seemed to distort degrees of cultural and political corruption and the cancerous gulf between the rich and the poor; worse, it tended to obscure the true power of mystery. The deeper ramifications of what was happening on the perilous paths of American experience seemed to elude many novelists; few appreciated the phenomenal increase in individual awareness that was creating a revolutionary change in consciousness, and dissolving the line between fact and fiction.

One of the first clients who came to the off-white living room in Cow Hollow was aware of change and consciousness. Doug Boyd had been a research assistant at the Menninger Foundation in Topeka, Kansas. Tall and confident and dressed in a beautiful saffron-colored shirt bought in Asia years before, he explained how he had been working with an American Indian medicine man, Rolling Thunder, and now wanted to write a book about the experience. I had learned to be cautious about publishing commitments, but that afternoon, intrigued by what I heard and read, I did not hesitate, and our agreement began a revision of personal priorities that would provide greater change than I could ever have imagined.

After returning from the Far East, Boyd had joined the Menninger Foundation in 1968. Assigned to a project called Voluntary Controls of Internal States, he had worked with Swami Rama, a Hindu adept, whose ability to demonstrate "psychophysiological self-regulation" was then being studied by Drs. Elmer and Alyce Green, world-famous pioneers in biofeedback research. It was in 1971, at a Third Annual Council Grove Conference, that Boyd first met Rolling Thunder. These events, sponsored by the Greens and held at White Memorial Camp in Council Grove, Kansas, drew professionals in psychology, medicine, religion, and science from all over the world, and were described by Alyce Green as attempts

> to cut across cultural boundaries, to look at contributions to the concept of consciousness by Zen Buddhism, Tibetan Buddhism, Integral Yoga, Sufism, Mystic Christianity, hypnosis, autogenic training, sensory deprivation, psychedelic-drug experience and biofeedback training.

Invited to speak, Rolling Thunder seemed to spend the first two days deciding whether he would. Boyd wrote that the medicine man wore "a red and white shirt with an Indian design, plain khaki pants and a brown hat with an eagle feather on it." When he finally reached the speaker's stand, he took a long, slow drink from a pop bottle and "set that down like the gentle tap of a gavel. The brown hat with the eagle feather stayed on his head." Rolling Thunder told of his apprenticeship to older medicine people and how, when he was young, he had traveled from reservation to reservation to learn and spend time with elders where

> sometimes we would sit in the sun all day long and never a word would be said. And I'd never question a medicine man because that's impossible. He would tell me what he wanted me to know.

Outlining seven basic types of disease and "many others from each of those," he said there were

> seven different rituals to go through before we cure any sickness or disease. In each of those rituals if you haven't purified yourself and if you don't approach the thing in the right way you're not going to make it.

This speech and a healing demonstration that followed so impressed Boyd that he followed the medicine man west and eventually came to me about publishing the results.

The project drew me into a vast network of inquiry that stretched beyond borders of ordinary concern. At the time I had little appreciation of the link between experience and consciousness; for the first forty-odd years of my life I had simply accepted experience as encounter or action that was more or less memorable. Ignorant of *other* dimensions, I dealt only with circumstance and, believing memory to be the only link with the past, engaged the future with innocent respect. In later years, whenever I looked back, I was always awed by how terribly unprepared I was for all that followed.

Everything seemed influenced by the impression of Rolling Thunder, and through this impression I began to realize the depth and breadth of the American emergency. It was repeatedly reflected in the struggle of traditional American Indians for preservation of their spiritual heritage, a recognized but poorly understood drama. Though their plight was assigned a place in the liberal conscience, no tangible relief came to those Indians who insisted on maintaining traditional roles and living old ways. In the public mind red people remained noble savages of the past, vaguely consigned to some historical limbo when, in fact, they were the original Americans, whose contemporary conditions were deplorable. Some positive economic change came to those American Indians who adapted to white ways, yet by 1980 the status of traditionals was more ambiguous than ever. The irony was that whenever Indian rights were defined, the definition was usually obscured by the Bureau of Indian Affairs or Bureau of Land Management. Their procrastinations and continually changing policies were usually excused as "regional mismanagement," but more dedicated observers suspected that such bungling was designed to combat one problem: traditional American Indians desired to retain treaty lands, which blocked the development of billions of dollars of natural resources contained in those lands.

Doug Boyd's book tried to reflect this. It documented the illegal destruction of sacred Shoshone piñon trees in Nevada by the Bureau of Land Management, and revealed ugly welfare injustices. Rolling Thunder was involved in these matters, for the actions of a medicine man or woman often had political consequences. I fathomed he did not relish such involvement and felt he would have been content to just hunt herbs, heal, and be free to attend to spiritual matters, leaving politics to tribal chiefs. But too many political problems involved the Earth, and for traditional Indians the Earth was spiritual.

Throughout the work on the Rolling Thunder project, I had a variety of new recognitions. I became aware not only of Rolling Thunder's shamanistic power—his ability to answer questions before they were asked, or arrive at the precise hour when he was most needed—but of the unforgettable effects of his *sense* of things. He was a soft-spoken man who enjoyed his pipe and tobacco; at the same time he was a tough human being whose poise exuded a subtle life force. Obviously bitter about the failure of white society to right the wrongs suffered by traditional Indians, he seemed to overcome this frustration by vision and the reaffirmation of ancient teachings. It surprised me to find that he was interested in white medicine. During one of his visits to Cow Hollow, he expressed admiration for what the white physician could accomplish, especially with surgery. At the same time he pitied the physician's greatest limitation—charging for services. Like the Sufi healer, who never accepted more than a handful of barley, the Indian healer asked for nothing and accepted only token gifts. Rolling Thunder never considered the white physician wrong, only ignorant, and believed that someday, "when more was known," the white physician would correct this fundamental error.

Although cynical of white liberals, Rolling Thunder was sympathetic with anyone who sought justice or change, even if that person was inspired by nothing more than the rejection of material values. He had an instinctual understanding of the vast extent of individual confusion among white people, but was encouraged by the growing ecological awareness among them, especially the young. In light of this, I once asked him if he thought the growing interest in human potential might bring some solution to the American problem as a whole. It was a lame question, and he was not impressed. He had just arrived from Carlin, Nevada, passing through San Francisco on his way to join other Indian activists to protest the arrest of an eighty-year-old medicine woman. Even though the off-white living room was crowded with others vying for his attention, after a minute or two of reflecting on my question, he turned to me and answered with his eyes, a means of communication at which he excelled. The look conveyed his belief that the white problem would not be solved by human potential, the white problem *was* human potential.

Only human beings have come to a point where they no longer know why they exist. They don't use their brains and they have forgotten the secret knowledge of their bodies, their senses, or their dreams. They don't use the knowledge the spirit has put in every one of them; they are not even aware of this, and so they stumble along blindly on the road to nowhere—a paved highway which they themselves bulldoze and make smooth so that they can get faster to the big, empty hole which they'll find at the end, waiting to swallow them up. . . . I have seen it. I've been there in my vision and it makes me shudder to think about it.

—Lame Deer

Published by Random House in 1974, the book on Rolling Thunder sold well, but by that time the association was involved with a growing number of projects—biographies, contemporary histories, photography, *Place* magazine, a quality paperback series of pure country opinion produced by a group of Whole Earth idealists working out of Walnut Creek, then a small delta community forty miles from San Francisco. In addition to this, we were all being drawn into an odd arena of new philosophy called New Age thought. Although engulfed in publishing problems—the most crucial of which was always the wavering line between costs and income—I became fascinated with the idea of a New Age and its concern with human potential and transformation—or the transformation of human potential. At first it all seemed to be little more than the anticipation of, or manipulation of, change. Instead of dutifully waiting for change, many of us were investigating and actively promoting ways and means it could be accelerated. Most felt accelerated change came out of the synergy of transformation of human potential, but more dedicated observers doubted that. Too often the idea of accelerated change was based only on intellectual or material measure, but these assumptions overlooked the fact that true change was the result of a unique awareness, or consciousness. Whatever the considerations, in those days few pronouncements fulfilled their promise, and wholesale excitement had to be tempered. I soon began to doubt any significant change could come from a kind of instant positivism that was a by-product of New Age philosophy, but my oldest friend, Crow, warned that my suspicion came from a failure to see that, whatever the source, a unique process of change had already begun.

Crow cautioned me to proceed carefully, saying that past a certain point of intrigue, I crossed the line of ordinary awareness, but, because of the confusion of common involvement—business pressures, child support, political irritations, the risk of romance, the cost of living, enigmatic people—identifying this line was extremely difficult. At that line awareness dissolved into mystery; there the limitlessness of consciousness began. Of course, this was not easy to understand, and time after time I tried to avoid the confusion by slipping into high highs, spirals in which change would change! Yet in the sober mornings after such exhilaration evaporated, I was drawn back to some common edge where it became necessary to begin again.

The worst obstacle to understanding seemed to be an inherited allegiance to the climate of materialism in which I had been bred; allegiance not totally purged by my earlier Beat refusal to conform, consent, or consume. I came to realize that I was still apprehensive of the *new,* and was continually lulled into believing that only established authority determined process or progress. But, after meeting Rolling Thunder, I began to recognize other ways that inspired me to go beyond old obstacles and beyond the fear that the new might prove to be old, after all. Ignorant of human potential and transformation, I had been trapped by that fear, which threatened anyone who chose to question traditional authority. Only because of the chaos of the 1950s and 1960s did this mindless rigidity begin to crumble, and only then could the image of Henry Cogdall, the private "who fell in the war for Wisdom," rise out of Spoon River to remind me that there could come a time "when crimes against culture / Will be punished the same as murder!"

Transformation was never easy. There was no recognizable turning point, no designated place to begin serious examination of awareness, or consciousness, and time after time I became deeply discouraged or embarrassed by the dead ends of naive enthusiasm. But I persevered and spent years working with unusual people who sacrificed much to confront problems that made revision of the human contract imperative. What was curious was that few of these individuals seemed cognizant of the ramifications of what they were doing. Most were satisfied not to be distracted from a particular passion or expertise, and many were hindered by the conviction that their own dedication to physics, healing, or parapsychology, or devotion to a religious figure (usually Eastern) encompassed the entire problem. They might sympathize with the need for a broad definition of diverse aspects of human potential, but they were content to ignore unification until they secured some immediate understanding of a particular specialty or exhausted existing grant money.

I had no such restrictions; that was both a blessing and a curse. Because of my literary and publishing background, which made me aware of a wide variety of philosophies and ways of life, I could see that diverse aspects had to be unified in order to produce whole pictures, and could see also that for this to happen I had to revise my scientific as well as spiritual beliefs.

During its first five years the association flourished—to a point. Supported by many whose needs were ruled by similar fascinations, it served as a critical focus for ideas and ideals. At the same time, mired in the business of the business, early idealism had to be sacrificed to the realities of deadlines, contracts, promotional responsibilities, and project decisions that could seldom be evaluated until eighteen to twenty-four months after a work was published. Even then judgment was difficult, for not every good book sells.

By 1975 New Age theaters had emerged, and their stages were crossed by scholars, utopians, and counterfeits of every stripe. Still, legitimate inquiry survived and there was credible progress. The most notable contributions were made by those who, rather than anguish over the supposition that America did not work, were determined to create positive change. These individuals felt it was foolish to lose faith or drop out, and even more foolish to flaunt real or imagined transcendence.

Year after year, one trip after another, I went to conferences, experiments, raps, and happenings along the New

Age theater circuit. I attended symposiums, games, Rolf-ings, and psychic massages held in institutes, ashrams, and centers; some programs were arduously crafted and others were rehashes of pirated doctrines.

And everywhere I went someone wanted to write a book or wanted to publish a work that would spread a message or bring fame or money or both. Because of this the association was provided an unusual entrée. As a publisher interested in the consciousness movement, it was easy to be invited backstage for a view off-limits to most others. Often I found publishable material, but no one capable of writing it, or capable writers without enough publishable material. The latter was usually the case. Despite the advent of the word processor, writing was still a laborious undertaking for which there was no guarantee of success. Few of those who intended to write ever began. Fewer finished. Only a fraction of those ever saw their work in print, and a still smaller number were rewarded with an audience, let alone royalties.

New Age writers were also prone to special problems. For one thing, contracted proposals could become dated in the year or two it took to write the book. For another, writers experienced unexpected conversions brought on by the effects of dealing with their particular subject matter; one critical study of Zen Buddhism was aborted when the writer suddenly moved to Japan. Worse, motivation might mysteriously dissipate in the process of exploring some edge of inquiry, or perspective would be distorted by the famous photograph of the whole Earth taken from space, an inspirational mirage that was more easily enjoyed than employed. Solid exposition might communicate facts but fail to convey the magic. The trouble was that the very *idea*

of consciousness was difficult to communicate and required continual modification. Initial investigations were
often frustrated by indecision or fear, until the writer
learned that fear usually preceded change while at the same
time creating the need for it. Heraclitus said that only
change endured, but in 1975 that did not answer the question of where or how to begin to break fixed patterns. Nor
did his words warn of the hidden paralysis of doubt that
could subvert desire, or expose the deceptive line between
apparent and true change.

After realizing all this, I was able to begin a process that
created a difference in my own life, yet I could not escape
the basic recognition that, no matter what my experience
or good or bad fortune, in order for true change to take
place, I had to turn *inward* to transcend common confusion. This *going within* proved to be the fundamental first
step, but nearly a decade would pass before I realized what
Theodore Roszak meant when he wrote that

> the fate of the soul is the fate of the social order; that
> if the spiritual within us withers so too will all the
> world we build around us.

How simple a world we build out of fierce intentions!
Like so many others, I hoped New Age concepts would
somehow deliver awareness of everything from ecology to
feminism, on neighborhood as well as global levels. To say
the least, this did not happen, though significant change did
occur. In psychology, new gestalt produced all kinds of in-
novative encounter. The holistic approach in medicine, especially when applied to stress-related disease, demanded
and eventually received serious attention. Spiritual revival
in the West was accompanied by increased interest in East-

ern philosophy and religious practice. In science, the fifty-year-old principle of uncertainty was neatly labeled the new physics and given a brilliant debut.

Despite these changes, it was continually disappointing the way America seemed to absorb the idea of transformation, or consciousness, and synthesize it into a kind of gross national achievement, and more disappointing how physical fitness, a primary factor in personal change, was so flagrantly merchandised. I had hoped interest in consciousness would prove to be some long-awaited elixir that would rejuvenate the American Dream, but that notion was overly idealistic. The whole show was neutralized by the marketing of trends that often reduced inquiry to fatuous fad. Many associates thought I was unduly pessimistic and failed to recognize the effects of consciousness on a society less inhibited and more willing to experiment in order to change. I was told to take heart at the number of people alarmed by the dangers of poor diet and stress, and concerned with the need for a new scientific paradigm.

I agreed but was apprehensive, knowing from my own experience that the realization of greater consciousness required a broad, practical approach. Change was strange. The excitement of vogues or trends would never overcome the disorienting side effects of exercise, diet, or meditative relaxation, and never anticipate the way the understanding of paradigm could lift the veil from a fraudulent way of life that a month or moment before had seemed so secure. I was unprepared for the way alternatives shed such strange light on my own sense of place in the neighborhood of those who shared my quest, as well as those who dismissed what I hoped to become. At different times the concern with consciousness caused me to question action or reaction to such an extent that I would do little more than fall back on the fascinations that had first inspired me. This was depressing, and there were times when I could no longer read manuscripts or discuss proposals far into the night. Priorities would dissolve. Mail, usually examined religiously every morning, would be set aside and the immediacy of the telephone ignored. Some days I would simply unplug the black root in order to do some simple yogic exercise or meditation, or walk through the half-deserted neighborhoods of the Marina Green to the edge of the blue bay. Some evenings, after the rush hour traffic had ended, I would drive through different districts of San Francisco and watch hills and neighborhoods flow over the windshield of the car before disappearing into the deep recesses of Golden Gate Park. Farther out, near the edge of the ocean, I would circle back through Pacific Heights or the eucalyptus groves of the Presidio army base. Occasionally the boom of a ceremonial cannon would punctuate the sunset, leaving huge scarlet and purple splashes of color over the western horizon. As night began to shroud the apartment buildings on Telegraph Hill, and lonely figures climbed the slanted sidewalks toward colored doorways, I would return home or stop in North Beach for dinner at the Washington Square, Little City, or Perry's, the only saloon in town that offered "The Star-Spangled Banner" on the jukebox. I would arrive home relieved that the day was over, and night would consign confusion to obscurity.

Despite such removal, mounting involvements complicated my responsibility to authors and associates, as well as publishers in New York and Boston who had contracted for books that I represented. Being involved in only six or eight projects a year, I was amazed by house editors who handled that number monthly and, one way or another, still dealt with the corporate restrictions under which they worked. This was often a creative accomplishment in itself. I was especially aware of this when I visited New York or Boston, where, outside of corporate authority, I was able to take stock of trends that affected publishing as well as the ultimate quality of the reading experience. Concerns with consciousness often clashed with the hard edge of business. Each year, as production, printing, and warehousing costs rose, the demand for a quicker return on advance money rose along with them. In light of this, it was difficult to expect the trade to sympathize with the confusion of consciousness. Had this been a more common conflict among my peers, there might have been hope for more understanding, but this problem resulted from investigations which were taking me into such unfamiliar areas as biofeedback, precognition, psychometry, altered states, bioenergetics, kundalini, and cosmology—inquiry I could never hope to completely understand. The obvious thing to do was to cut down on the number of projects I was involved in, but because of previous commitments this proved unrealistic. Crow felt my concern was pointless "in the larger scheme of things," an insinuation he refused to explain at the time. But I had known Crow too long to expect explanations. When we met in Greenwich Village in the early 1950s, he was already a master at deflating dull drama, and because of this skill, had, over the years, become something of a part-time doppelgänger to those for whom he cared. Sprawled near the fluted fireplace, unusually relaxed, except for his quick brown eyes, he ran his lean hand over his sharp jaw as he suffered my continuous complaints. The concern with consciousness was certainly the greatest demand I had ever made on our relationship; however, I knew that despite his sometimes pompish evasions, the potential of consciousness was something for which he held profound respect.

In trying to understand consciousness, I started by setting aside such issues as a new scientific paradigm or the mystery of telepathy and concentrating on the nature of individual awareness. This required the actualization of *going within* and began with simple physical and psychological self-improvement. Faced with the prospect of fitness, I became painfully aware of how woefully out of condition I was and how far I had fallen. Initial efforts at exercise were shocking, and attempts to control diet and consumption were embarrassing. In 1972 I could hardly run 100 yards before returning home stunned by my lack of stamina and my body's inability to respond to exertion. When it came to diet, my first fast turned into a seventeen-hour fiasco that ended before a wide-open refrigerator where I ate so much cold chicken I could not sleep. My first venture into meditation was equally unsuccessful: I could not sit still for five minutes, let alone thirty.

I despaired.

What was I trying to prove?

Was I out to make a new man of myself?

Yet I would not give up. Evidence in favor of exercise, diet, and relaxation was undeniable. So I continued—and failed—and began again, until slowly, after a time, I began to lose weight, sleep better, and recognize how ruinous middle-aged limitations had become. Finally, after weeks of rising at dawn, the thin framework of a larger scheme did evolve. Running became a source of energy, the practice of sane consumption a magnificent obsession, and meditative relaxation a royal release.

Still, there were constant complications. I had little trouble quitting tobacco, but the real problem was coffee, an onerous habit I began as a boy in Omaha, when it complemented homemade glazed donuts on cold winter mornings. By the time I reached college, coffee had become a refresher for round-the-clock rap sessions. In the late 1940s, when I first drank espresso at the Cafe Reggio in Greenwich Village, the taste was fatally fixed. Twenty years later I was addicted. I owned a large Chemex coffeemaker and used only bottled spring water and dated filter paper, storing sacks of French roast and Arabian mocha in the freezer. It was not unusual to begin a day with five or six black cups, followed by a fresh pot in the late afternoon, and more (maybe touched with brandy) late at night. This continued until 1972, when the first nutritional evaluations of caffeine crossed my desk in Cow Hollow. As evidence of the danger mounted, I found it ghoulish to drink the stuff while editing proof that stated coffee was as poisonous to the system as the white sugar with which it was sweetened.

I was not naive about the illusion of habit; still, I never looked on coffee or white sugar as particularly addictive. But, aware of the suburbs of addiction, I had to admit the vile sauce seemed to stain my soul. Repeated attempts to cut down failed, and the more I exercised and improved my diet, and the further I unified meditative relaxation, the more acute the need became. Eventually I realized I had to will a positive change and not simply fight a negative habit. But even this realization remained dormant until one brilliant morning, after a long run and short meditation, when—after I had gone into the kitchen and mechanically boiled spring water and folded a filter—I suddenly slipped into an odd release that ruptured the stranglehold of addiction. Slowly I shut off the gas burner and walked back into the wide living room, where, with no particular crescendo, I quit coffee. But that evening I felt bad, and later that night I was ill. The next day I could not function. From the back of my mouth down through the base of my stomach weird biles soured my body. Quitting coffee became an exorcism rather than rejuvenation, and had all the signs of withdrawal—the same horribly funked reaction that comes from cleansing the body of ugly matter. The worse reaction seemed to stem from a residue of oil and acidity throughout the digestive system rather than any grip of caffeine, a misery that was doubly upsetting because it was so unexpected. On the third day I was able to rise out of bed. By the end of the week, when the last of an obnoxious acidity slick passed through my system, I felt well enough to work, but it was more than a month before I regained a decent equilibrium.

The world is not a "prison house" but a kind of spiritual kindergarten where millions of bewildered infants are trying to spell "God" with the wrong blocks.
                        —Edwin Arlington Robinson

At least twice every year I flew back to New York to call on publishers and visit my father who, since the death of my mother in 1973, had begun writing longer letters, reading more newspapers, eating more of his meals out. Every time the jumbo jet circled over the edge of the Atlantic, I would peer out the window in the hope of seeing the Manhattan skyline, but usually had to settle for the grayish edges of Rockaway Beach or the massive red blocks of Long Island apartment houses before the landing gear bumped on the runway. Disappointment would be quickly forgotten in the rattling taxi ride over the Triborough Bridge under which an East River barge floated below skeletons of new high-rise construction. Once, in a nostalgic mood, I asked a driver if the White Horse Tavern was still on Hudson Street or had they torn that down too? Welded to the wheel, he ignored the question and expected to be forgiven the discourtesy, so I did not bother to tell him that I usually stayed with friends on East 89th Street and looked forward to morning walks down Madison Avenue to meet with editors, publicists, and salespeople. Obviously he would not have appreciated the delight I found in antique shop windows and galleries or the gushing rides up stainless steel elevators where, pinned behind a loving grin of a paraplegic messenger or assorted fellow travelers, I would rehearse what I should say and try to remember what I should not. After five or six years of these visits, I instinctively knew who to call on, and after the third or fourth breakfast, lunch, or dinner, what I did not need to eat.

Such were the times.

I was always more or less welcomed, because better editors in New York houses valued comments from any region in the country and particularly California. With few exceptions I profited from my contacts, even the educational rejection the day before the exhilaration of a successful deal.

Toward the end of each week, I would allow myself the leisure of wandering through midtown neighborhoods to while away time between appointments. In the Barclay Hotel I would lounge in the lobby and listen to the exotic birds sing under a magnificent stained glass cage. Sitting on blue divans in the Waldorf Astoria, I would make visual studies of foreigners, matching faces or language with imaginary assignations. Once, in the basement of the Metropolitan Museum, I spent two hours circling huge glass display cases full of historically poised mannequins dressed in Russian *War and Peace* costumes, until a strange déjà vu forced me outdoors, where I sat on the broad stone steps and listened to the music of the water fountains splash with the clash of traffic . . . before strolling down 5th Avenue to meet a friend from the trade at the Algonquin Hotel . . . where, alone on a soft sofa, I wondered if, during the

1930s, the better hours of the famous literary Round Table took place in the Pergola or the Rose Room . . . and where I pondered the question of whether the American novel could be critically divided between the cosmopolitan Atlantic and the provincial Pacific oceans. Since I had left Columbia University twenty-five years before, I had reached no conclusions, and on every visit since, the dimension of the question had shrunk . . . as I divined less and less from the fading pattern of the worn carpets and the timeless tables and lumpy furniture . . . even when it began to rain or when someone quietly laid a Reserved sign against the belly of the sleeping cat who curled on a corner rocker. When the blur of my friend's gray overcoat appeared, I recalled Crow's speculation that the problem of the American novel was that it had become limited by linear vision. The modern novel failed to capture contemporary life, he insisted, because too few novelists were influenced by attitudes and circumstances of their previous lives.

"Don't you see," he explained, "leftover experience from past lives explains multiplicity of personality and accounts for all kinds of behavior, even the schizophrenic refuge! In the modern novel, action and reaction will have to consider the conflicts of previous lives which were never resolved or were aborted—lives that continue to prejudice the living present. Until the novelist sees the composition of lives, the novel will never fully reflect who we are or why we lead these partial lives! Novelists still draw fictional characters from archaic psychoanalytic models. That's not only linear, its myopic!"

All of these reflections conflicted with the meeting at hand. I wanted to say something about the modern novel, to explain Crow's opinion that past genders filtered through and confused the present. I longed to ask whether we simultaneously lived more lives—or selves—than we knew, but the question was lost in the five o'clock cocktail din and the reality of the publishing trade. Soured by his day, my friend was badly in need of a drink. Only that morning a highly respected editor in chief from a large house had been told to be out of his building by noon and, as the news of this firing spread, those in publishing who deplored this kind of senseless corporate hatchet job were revolted and more upset than ever over the fate of good books. Joined by three partisans from a nearby table, we drank to the plight of serious writing before turning to other gossip, deals, and an evaluation of tomorrow's appointments.

Oddly enough, the next day, at an expensive restaurant, my host was especially cheerful. He had just been promoted by the same house that had evicted the editor in chief the day before, and was very enthusiastic about finally getting a list together "that will really reflect where things are really at!"

I promptly agreed and, fortunately without having to explain what I meant, announced that modern times required that all of us go beyond dated Freudian determinism. On that oblique note, we opened huge red menus and ordered lunch and a fine Italian white wine.

I passed the bread, ignored the butter, and began to do what I had set out to do—sell the man an eight-page proposal for an excellent overview of humanistic psychology I had mailed from San Francisco the week before. My host was well read in the field and aware of the psychology market, but also quite frank about the "uneven sales of too much of this kind of stuff."

I only insisted the consciousness market should not be measured by past trends. I warned that "consciousness is more of a process than a product" and would ultimately come to change the very fiber of American life . . . pointing out how books on holistic medicine, once considered faddish, now sold extremely well. He agreed but seemed unimpressed. Inspired by the wine, I went on to argue how consciousness would ultimately come to be the deciding factor in the current ecological crisis; not only of the Earth but the body and spirit as well. I even predicted how consciousness might well become the energy behind a true spiritual revival—the signs were everywhere. These claims were high but I believed them. Yet conviction had little to do with the fact that even an overview of humanistic psychology would ultimately have a profit-and-loss statement for which the purchasing editor would be partially responsible. We agreed that to have an appreciable sale in cloth and do well in trade paperback, the work would have to withstand academic criticism. I felt the proposed book would do that and still introduce the reader to futuristic aspects of the mind/body/spirit relationship. Had I stopped there, I might have made a deal.

Perhaps I was still affected by the *War and Peace* costumes or the linear limitations of the modern novel or the wine. In any case, I made the mistake of introducing the "limitlessness of consciousness," which at the time so fascinated me. Failing to notice a pause across the table, I talked about the day when we would see more in the relationship between mind and body. I said that the day was near when we would realize whole new worlds that were obscure now . . . when we would come to comprehend the neurology of the aura, an accomplishment that would lead us to understand the psychic system from which romantic and spiritual attachments originate.

At "neurology of the aura," the air thickened, and my host lowered a forkful of expensive green peas with the ease only a highly paid executive could affect. Of course the deal was off, the wine unfinished, and my confidence in the limitlessness of consciousness suspended until the following morning, when I sold the proposal to another editor, who did not have time for lunch.

That afternoon it rained, so I went into a delicatessen near 50th Street and 3rd Avenue and ate a bowl of clam chowder. There an elderly waitress, Rose, sensing my peculiar dislocation, repeatedly filled my water glass and assured me the weather would change.

It did.

Two hours before my flight, the sun came out and I stood on the curb to enjoy the wondrous whirl of New York that rose off the asphalt and swirled about the passing people and rumbling trucks . . . a unique folk music found only in that part of Manhattan, where I reluctantly flagged another rattling taxi to the airport.

Popular flights to California left Kennedy Airport in the late afternoon and, with the three-hour time difference, arrived in San Francisco in early evening after passing over a middle America that looked like a patchwork quilt of complementary place mats. The trip was always tiring, but coming home somehow eased the tension of failure and success and dissolved the soft fatigue I felt at the top of the stairs. Setting down the suitcase, I would poke at my pile of mail or shuffle through a messy stack of telephone messages. Once, before going into the bedroom to unpack, I felt a powerful desire to turn back and descend the stairs in order to lose myself in some lovely blurred meadow that would disappear immediately if given further credence. After a long moment the sensation passed. I heard the doorbell ring just as the tardy cat slipped through the half-opened window and demanded to be fed.

It is dangerous to confess spiritual poverty, for whoever is poor has cravings and whoever craves draws his fate upon himself.

—*Jung*

On my fiftieth birthday, I walked along a beach in Monterey, unable to assimilate the impact of living a half-century. It was a lovely morning. The jagged coastline matched its white sand and massive rocks against the reverential green of the pines high on the hills behind me, and shifting breakers seemed able to translate designs of the past into the present. Misery and mistakes of the past were flushed by the foam into forgiving visualizations—long, ironic progressions from the Depression years of the 1930s through the forty years of economic recovery that followed, almost a historic lottery of opportunity. Out of all that had happened in the fifty years, war and technology were the most memorable. In my life so much had come so soon and often that I was never able to completely assess, only adjust to change no one seemed fully to understand. I realized how, decade after decade, in the wake of revolving prosperity and cultural upheavals, I had come to resent prophetic pronouncements that I was entering a glorious Space Age. It was a promise that permeated everyone's thinking, though few knew what it meant. Too many forces were beyond public control and there were too many paradoxes: industrial waste seeped out of the ground, yet responsible officials often disguised the cause. Futurists promised extraterrestrial colonies, yet rail and bus transportation were deplorable. Trillions of dollars were spent on militarism that afforded less and less protection; murder rates doubled; school systems went bankrupt; and farm yields exceeded historical record, while millions suffered from a lack of wholesome food or any decent food at all. I could never decide if this was the fallout of progress or the sins of vested interest. Whatever the source, it couldn't be ignored. That day in Monterey, I was not only a disenchanted liberal but a fifty-year-old figure on a beach who instinctively knew that in order to do more than just survive, I would have to guard the hope of larger life and avoid the invisible suppression that threatened to bury me in ambiguous submission. There on one edge of the Pacific, I realized ordinary journeys were over. The only new frontier was within.

It had been wise to get away from the city that day; six hundred months should never be celebrated, only studied. Later that afternoon I enjoyed some delicious roast chicken and figs and a Heitz chardonnay while reviewing what had been accomplished by my zealous faith in change. All of the old cosmic doubts danced by. Was I running from middle age? Deceiving maturity with diet or avoiding modern stress with ancient revelations? No, no, the cynicism paled. In the past seven years my psychophysiological condition had radically improved. I could see and feel the difference and compare it against the aging of many contemporaries, yet there was still a questionable haze. New Age interest in consciousness had opened my mind to ways that secured escape from many exacting tolls, but I knew the advantage was thin and would have to carry me far beyond common vanity, certainly beyond demands of fitness and diet, if I hoped to reach the point where confusion dissolved and meaningful recognition began.

There were troubling considerations. The New Age had begun to elicit negative reaction. Many critics felt a search for greater consciousness demanded such excessive attention to personal concern that it exaggerated self-importance and became hopelessly narcissistic. Though indiscriminate extremes could lead to fruitless exhibitionism and painful dead ends, I was convinced that serious seekers could go beyond such obstacles, and suspected that much criticism of New Age ideals was often little more than the calculated counterattack of conventional watchdogs who instantly responded to any threat to the status quo. Unfortunately, there were deplorable acts in New Age theaters. All kinds of sarcastic delight could be found in the garish attention given gnarled gurus, the clumsy bounce of the overweight jogger, and the naive understanding of the implications of quantum physics and uncertainty.

The most incisive criticism came from Christopher Lasch, an academic who found little human potential in the cultural changes that had begun in the 1950s. Lasch charged that the consciousness movement amounted to little more than a self-preoccupation that addressed trivial or unreal issues and provided self-defeating solutions. Writing in the *New York Review of Books* in September 1976, he said the consciousness movement rose out of "a perverse dissatisfaction with the quality of personal relations" and that it advised people "not to make too large an investment in love and friendship, to avoid excessive dependence on others and to live for the moment."

It was a kind of indictment popular with conservatives, because it was the most sweeping condemnation that could be made against behavioral trends that threatened traditional materialism or monogamy. The conservative personality could seldom appreciate the nature of increased awareness or radical removal, or comprehend the freedom and growth that could develop because of it. And because it was so sweeping, the criticism was indiscriminate. Before 1950 the idea of consciousness was hardly recognized in America, but by the 1970s it was available to anyone willing to revise his or her way of life in order to achieve other levels of understanding. There was no question that a longing for increased awareness could arise from a "dissatisfaction with the quality of personal relations," but this was because traditional relations were sometimes so limiting they became unbearable. I came to believe that by carefully *going within*, a concerned individual could develop the discipline to do far more than "live for the moment." Going within could help a person demand (and, in turn, give) nothing less than a positive, loving response and, when diligently pursued, issues that may have seemed trivial or unreal gained other kinds of importance never before imagined.

Crow simply dismissed the criticism, reminding anyone who would listen that Narcissus was only a male model who refused offers of love, refused even the heart of the lovely Echo, the mountain nymph who pined for him until only her voice remained. "How would that apply now? Before Echo would pine away, she'd begin to pity Narcissus—or suspect he was gay—and hang around to find out if his reflection in the pool differed from recent photographs. She'd want to know whether the savages were right in fearing that cameras rob parts of the soul! Oh, don't be taken in, old man. The charge of narcissism is just a clever way to sow doubt, get an audience, or maybe win another grant. Actually, it's only a koan in the back room of Zen!"

As the sun sank into the Pacific, the beach turned cool. At the end of the next cove, a group of gulls flew over the quivering foam that separated the water and the rising moon. Crow's reaction provided some comfort, but it did not solve the problem that, in seeking greater consciousness, I still had nowhere to begin—no definitive point at which I could find an acceptable order of consideration. There was no prospectus, no map.

In the following months I withdrew and began to search for ways to create my own order out of all I had learned. First of all, it seemed necessary to modulate fascination, and formulate some basic order that would help me to avoid subjugating the self to any particular intellectual or spiritual promises produced in New Age theaters. Since 1972 I had experienced too much not to be suspicious of those who insisted it was absolutely necessary to follow one specific discipline or denomination in order to achieve greater consciousness. Certainly there was a need to be familiar with the implications of uncertainty and holism, just as there was a need to realize the importance of Buddhism, Zen, or the benefits of silence; but before accepting any idea or ideal, the individual first had to reclaim the self that was trapped in a misused body or an inebriated or neglected mind. Above all, he or she had to avoid situations where passionate interest in the prowess of powerful per-

sonalities led to an exploitation of the paralyzing awe suffered by those who were drawn toward the unknown. The
person who skipped any of these initial steps ran the risk
of having no inner presence on which to rely, no sense of
things that would instinctively recoil from intimidating
confusion. I had seen too many unfortunates sorting out
garbled transmission—common and cosmic—and too
many Gita-grunting disciples pinned under the rim of im-
ported mystical toes not to believe otherwise. Still, by the
end of the first week, all I had accomplished was a partial
list of what I considered to be important areas of
understanding:

- the uncertainty principle
- the philosophical implications of uncertainty
- chronic stress
- the mind/body problem
- the hologram
- effects of questionable diet
- bioenergetics
- split-brain research
- economic anxiety (or materialistic constipation)
- psychosynthesis
- spiritual poverty
- religious revival
- tantrism
- debased sensory/conceptual input
- astrology
- emotional anatomy
- yoga
- ecological crises

The effort disclosed the enormous journey that I would
have to make for a comprehensive understanding of con-

sciousness. The enormity punctured more of my New Age idealism; at the same time it shed sober light on the need to break through inherited patterns—the need to shred the fabric of ordinary awareness and the need to act *into* something.

I don't remember when I first thought about giving a silent dinner party, but once I entertained the idea, it would not be dismissed. I felt that some kind of removal might come out of inviting a few select people to supper with the stipulation that there be no conversation. I was divorced at the time, a weekend father, and the demands of living and working in the same house caused me to vacillate for weeks before I was finally able to make a list of those who would be attuned to the idea. These seven people had been over a month before, so to recreate a comfortable situation, I served the same meal: Irish stew, sourdough bread, zinfandel, and Häagen-Dazs ice cream. I forgot to serve a salad and no one seemed to notice, but the next day I realized that no one could have mentioned it anyway.

The early arrivals opened the wine, played records, and smiled as they passed cheese and celery. Two particulars mugged and clowned a bit while lighting some marijuana. There was some initial humorous banter, but after the awkwardness wore off the group fell into a sweet, sane state and a unique peace came over the evening.

No one spoke.

It worked.

It created a difference.

Simple gestures were sufficient to seat everyone at the table and to signal when anyone wanted a dish passed. I was astonished by the ease with which we communicated without speaking. What was also apparent was how imprisoned we had become; how wired into the patterns of

polite behavior and the petty obligations of instantly eval-
uating remarks and replying to meaningless banter. Relieved of the obligation to listen, free of the traffic of the
mouth, we seemed paroled into a new, different atmosphere where we were able to feel and share our actions. At
the same time, anyone could recede into private reflection
where impressions and comparisons became more vivid as
the evening wore on. When it came time to leave, no one
spoke. As people departed they shook hands and a few
hugged, but most were content to exchange looks.

Over a period of several months, I gave three more silent
dinners for smaller groups. As far as I was concerned, each
succeeded the other in bridging borders of awareness and
revealing recognitions previously obscured. The evenings
were rare enough to weather the wag who thought the evening worthwhile for no other reason than it "kept Briggs
quiet for a whole night," and rare enough to disregard the
charge that it was self-centered of me to arrange the evenings exclusively around my particular friends and associates. Even Crow felt some strangers should be included,
but he was the first to admit something important occurred. For the first time it was possible to realize other
feelings of experience—to see otherness as some extension,
some uncharted area of reality that was seemingly always
a bit beyond the limits of ordinary understanding. Before
the silent dinners, otherness had been little more than
vague, esoteric expectation or a particular world of isolated
intuitive insight; as I became more adept at utilizing the
freedom of silent company, I seemed able to recapture a
sense of time, a sense of larger life that had been lost in the
tyranny of common conversation.

After an hour or so, faces and figures began to change,
fade, or gain curious significance, often evolving forgotten

familiarity or characteristics out of what could have been strange cousins from the past or a past before that. Occasionally an individual whose relationship to me was rather mundane would turn into a divided presence—a different edition of the same figure. Often pairs or trios transposed into ancient tableaux near the long black couch, or a single silhouette might pass the crooked bookcase near the tall brass lamp . . . disappearing between shadows of memory of ten years or fifty, or a hundred years before that. The evenings were a kind of silent theater, living film so uniquely set they gave rise to foreign focus. Once, in the hall, a man and woman paused near a dark oval table to exchange glances and chemistry. Ordinarily such chance encounter would have gone unnoticed by me, because of all the hackneyed conversation that mushroomed out of tight greetings, hilarious asides, and smoked flattery, but the silent difference transfigured the pair. Across the way, three women instinctively grasped the difference of the evening and generated serious attention toward all that was usually diluted in mindless recitals of political outrage, fabulous bargains, the fate of children, or the potency of some celluloid celebrity about whom no one really cared. Observing all of the variations of all of the evenings, I began to suspect that memory did more than remember; it fused the past with the present and affected the future.

At the last supper it rained. Ignoring the four who had come to dinner that night, I stood at one of the twin windows, watching wet cars glide on the street below. After a few minutes the rain slowed time enough for me to admit that not everyone was as moved or removed by silent dinners as I was. Silence was not a popular American condition. Some might have been receptive to the idea of otherness, but it was rarely discussed, and I had no desire to find out by whom or how much. There was no need. The silent dinners—they could have been lunches or picnics, even silent affairs—had another advantage. I was able to take a longer look at the confusion of consciousness that a few months before had been highlighted by my attempt to list important areas of understanding; now, as I studied the wet street below, bits and pieces of obvious patterns began to revolve around four sides of the same image. The image began to produce a series of rectangles, each rectangle cut into four smaller rectangles. Within an hour these simple quartets revealed a kind of progressive understanding.

A fundamental quartet of individual reality

mind	body
spirit	environment

could be transposed into a quartet of individual concerns

conduct	health
faith	ecology

each concern being the domain of one of four basic disciplines

psychology	medicine
religion	science

The last quartet was especially intriguing, but I had to spend several minutes staring at it before I realized how, in innumerable ways, modern life was defined by this quartet and consequently contained within its limits. Within those limits an individual was a pinned and wriggling specimen, subjected to spheres of influence that were supposedly benign, even essential to personal well-being, and objective. The visualization was exciting and vivid, but two things were wrong: I was that individual and not all of that influence was benign or objective. No, three things were wrong! Not only was I wriggling beneath the influence of these four disciplines, and not only was the benignity and objectivity of the influence questionable, but that influence was a dominant authority over my life.

The realization deserved a finer moment than it received, for just at that moment two cars glided by and, maneuvering for the right of way, began honking at one another. This jolted me to yet another problem—the erroneous popular belief that the collective wisdom of modern psychology, medicine, religion, and science produced a kind of benevolent syncretism, an integrated understanding of the human condition. By 1980 this simply was not so. There was little syncretism in disciplines. Psychology, medicine, religion, and science had become elaborate domains, and each had politicized its own academic and professional importance and zealously demanded independent authority. The degree of interdisciplinary exchange was not only inconsequential, but was hampered by the hauteur of specialization that had been carried to extremes. *Worst of all, within each discipline was a destructive schism.*

Simply seen, psychology was bitterly split between behaviorism and humanism. Medicine was divided between strict treatment or pathology and a more preventive, holistic approach to health and healing. Religion was divided by dogma and mystery, and in science the implications of new discoveries in quantum physics had not been reconciled with traditional mechanistic determinism. This was easily visualized:

Psychology	Medicine
behaviorism/humanism	*pathology/prevention*
Religion	Science
dogma/mystery	*uncertainty/determinism*

Schisms were not new, of course. The struggle between

conformity and deviation was ageless, but by 1980 the iso-
latory effects of disciplinary specialization had become an
obstacle to integrated understanding. Claims of objectivity
were flawed by an inordinate importance given to parts.
Wholeness seemed suspended; as a consequence the well-
being of the individual seemed to be ignored. As the rain
continued to fall, I wondered if this was the reason that
people grasped at ways to attain human transformation—
through Zen, astrology or the Tao. Was this the reason
people jogged, avoided white sugar, or fasted with such
studied concentration? Or why so many reverently tended
house plants or rashly dropped alcoholic friends who
smoked—all the while wondering whether the foreign gurus had better answers?

As the rain let up, I wondered whether the human condition had been misappropriated by arrogant rationalists,
and recalled dialogue and warnings about the negative effects of specialization. Before I could dwell on this issue, I
turned and discovered the living room was empty. My
guests were gone.

Within the publishing association the schisms attracted
more attention than the quartets themselves. In the off-
white living room, one associate agreed the idea of the
quartets was rewarding, but felt it was dangerous to sim-
plify the issue of consciousness. "Besides, you've allowed
no place for the philosopher! What's more, you have to face
the fact that not all of behaviorism, pathology, dogma, and
determinism is obsolete."

That was true; I maintained, however, that although
New Age thought regarding consciousness had been created out of cross-disciplinary comparison, in academia the

perception of consciousness had been obscured, if not purposely ignored, by specialization and disciplinary isolation. I also knew many intelligent individuals who believed disciplinary schisms to be little more than different schools of thought, often inspired by research and, as a consequence, beneficial to some ultimate understanding. The drawback of specialization was that it tended to reinforce fixed belief systems and support the labyrinth of authority needed to manage such systems. This created a maze of complicated intellectual and technological patronage that not only resisted change but, for obvious reasons, resisted the examination of radical ideas. The oft-used example was that if humanistic psychology ever replaced behaviorism in official institutional favor, the turnover in university positions alone would be devastating to thousands of reputations, and the cost in textbook replacement would be staggering.

The same astute associate also felt that the terms needed clarification. "The schism between pathology and prevention might be more accurately depicted as being between surgical/pharmaceutical intervention and prevention. Of course the problem is that surgical/pharmaceutical intervention is so tragically tied to vast systems of health insurance and hospitalization that to reduce its prominence through the awareness of prevention might well affect the economic balance of the whole medical/pharmaceutical complex—something the present medical establishment would deny.

"And here in religion, your schism between dogma and mystery should be between dogma and transcendence, which better compares contemporary religious problems. In the Christian dogma of creation, nature existed primarily for the *use* of humans, a fact which has been seen by some thinkers as the source of this century's ecological crises.

"And the schism between uncertainty and determinism might be more accurately labeled freedom and determinism, because, oddly enough, uncertainty leads to freedom." Didn't I know that?

Yes, I did. I also knew that any comparative study of determinism and uncertainty was complicated, and that, in 1980, though few scientists would have called themselves determinists, determinism lived on in many guises—behaviorism, Freudianism, and Marxism were only three. Though defunct as a universal paradigm, determinism obviously retained some applications. I also knew the philosopher Arthur Young insisted that the existence of freedom in no sense negated but, in fact, paralleled the determinate world of molar particles which we inhabit in our waking lives. This intriguing idea was one of many reasons why the work of Arthur Young was imporant to a comprehensive understanding of consciousness.

*If the nineteenth century is to be governed by the
opinions of the eighteenth, and the twentieth by
the nineteenth, the world will always be governed
by dead men.*

       —Elizabeth Cady Stanton

An American born in Paris at the turn of the century, Arthur Middleton Young exhibited unusual curiosity right from the start. As a child he tried to discover "who was God's nurse?" Later, in his third year at Princeton University, he requested a course in relativity; when the request was granted, he was the only student. Although attracted to philosophy, Young decided in 1928 to learn to solve problems to which answers could be tested, and devoted himself to private research on the helicopter. More than a decade later, with the outbreak of World War II, he patented his ideas and went to Bell Aircraft. After the war, in 1947, his Model 47 was awarded the world's first commercial helicopter license. Stunned by Hiroshima, Young left Bell to return to philosophy and to continue work on a theory of process he had begun years before. His original interest in the helicopter had grown into the idea of the psychopter, "the winged self." In 1952 he set up the Foundation for the Study of Consciousness in Philadelphia to develop a theory of process that "recognized scientific laws but also gave sanction to realities not subject to the laws of determinism, such as free will and psychic phenomena." Twenty years later he came to California and opened the Institute for the Study of Consciousness in Berkeley. By this time his theory was contained in two major works, *The Reflexive Universe* and *The Geometry of Meaning*, books that had taken more than fifteen years to complete and for which I arranged publication in 1976.

I was not the only person impressed with Arthur Young, an elegant visionary who long before had resigned himself to patient understanding. It was said he was continually trying to deal with solutions before most people realized there was a problem. Nevertheless, recognition of his work did begin. In 1984, thirty-seven years after it went into production, the Bell Model 47, which combined Young's design of the bubble canopy with the open structure of the tail boom, was put on permanent exhibition in the Museum of Modern Art in New York.

Many times after a trip to New York, I would ride worn Amtrak trains through Philadelphia to Downington, Pennsylvania, where Young spent his summers and where we would indulge in conversations that were as varied as they were unpredictable. One September evening, while enjoying drinks on the patio and observing the lush change of summer into autumn, I complained that although I believed the recognition of greater consciousness contained "the modern solution," the realization seemed hampered by the fact that consciousness had never been adequately defined. Because it was too late to discuss such a complex problem, we rose to go inside for dinner, pausing to enjoy the sunset over the greenish brown hills. When we did the rutting roar of a motorcycle ripped the valley below. While the noise groaned on in the distance, Arthur, unperturbed, opened the door and murmured, "Consciousness is what you need when things don't work."

Colin Wilson considered *The Reflexive Universe* "a breathtaking experience." In it Young theorized the universe was put into motion by purpose, and saw the evolution of the universe as a process rather than a structure. *The Reflexive Universe* showed the place of humanity in relationship to the rest of nature. Based on science as well as mysticism, it made a crucial distinction between the physical world, which could be observed and measured, and inner experience—such as thought, value, and soul—which could not. This theory of process, made possible by the new discoveries of quantum physics, included not only modern science but ancient teaching, myth, and religion, and drew a fascinating correlation between physics and the spiritual core of the universe. Such correlation had been introduced in the late 1960s and brilliantly popularized in the 1970s by Fritjof Capra in *The Tao of Physics*. But *The Reflexive Universe* went a great deal further, for Young's theory of process offered a new paradigm. Kenneth Pelletier wrote that

> No accounting of the empirical data of science or the metaphors of mythology would add up to a complete description of reality without addressing itself to the proposition that the universe itself is in the process of evolution. Arthur Young has accomplished the formidable task of articulating a paradigm of a dynamic reflexive universe wherein science and mysticism, data and values, structure and purpose equally coexist.

Process was the essence of Young's paradigm and could be seen as the logical bridge between the obsolescence of determinism and the freedom of uncertainty. Such theory was complex; nevertheless neither critic nor convert could ignore complexity, yet this complexity was the source of modern confusion. Whereas on the one hand, consciousness—knowing through instinct or intuition—was a remedy for the conflicting influences the individual was subjected to, on the other hand, it so ruptured old belief systems that it caused many to yearn for the traditional authority determinism supposedly provided, and, in turn, caused others to recoil in frustration when forced to rely on specialized authority for explanation or interpretation of individual well-being.

The critical question was whether we had innocently consigned our individual well-being to the wrong forces. Splintered by schisms, established disciplines began to seem like deceptive mirrors. In psychology who could one turn to—the behaviorist or the humanist? In medicine should one rely on pathology or prevention? Should one bow to religious dogma or begin individual exploration into spiritual mystery? And what were the effects of uncertainty on lifestyle? Once read and understood, *The Reflexive Universe* was invaluable in addressing these questions, for it incorporated purpose into human evolution by demonstrating that life required, "in addition to materials and conditions, an act of will."

I mentioned to Crow that will—the power of volition—was the key to overcoming the confusion of consciousness; it was the fuel of purpose.

"Quite true, but that doesn't *explain* the confusion. The New Age has failed to publicly define uncertainty. What uncertainty is to the scientist is not what uncertainty is to the individual. To the scientist uncertainty represents freedom, but to your concerned individual, straining for psychological as well as physical well-being, the idea of uncertainty is the motif of the twentieth century, and a potential source of totalitarianism! The disintegration of authority—the holocaust, the sexual revolution, crippling stress—seems to be produced by uncertainty. For the truly concerned individual, the split is not between uncertainty and determinism, but between freedom and sane survival. Science is not life! Yet science is so revered that it no longer feels it is necessary to submit to human reality. Why should it? For more than a hundred years it has dazzled civilization with material rewards and heroes—from Newton to Einstein, from Pasteur to Freud. Waving test tubes and technology, science has buried ancient wisdom and probably, in effect, brought about global crisis. Now, in the twentieth century, it has saved itself from deterministic extremes with uncertainty, but it can't advertise the salvation because the implication of uncertainty is freedom—even from science!"

He went on, but the further he went the more obscure he became about the importance "of recognizing and recovering the primordial need of transcendence!" Modern confusion, he said, was "the failure of science to admit mystery." Mystery was still "the grand power, despite multimillion-dollar grants that most scientists believed were given on intellectual merit alone." This might have been so, but I felt that true comprehension of consciousness was impossible without understanding the implications of uncertainty and free will. So in the following weeks I started to research uncertainty; it proved to be a long examination.

In 1927 Werner Heisenberg's uncertainty principle shattered the popularly held idea that if cause were known, effect could be predicted. Einstein rejected uncertainty with the famous comment that he did not believe God played dice with the universe. But even if God did not gamble, the philosophical implications of uncertainty effectively ended the domination of determinism that had grown out of Newtonian physics and, according to Arthur Young, had given

> science its *first comprehensive theory* and laid the basis of the billiard ball hypothesis, the belief that the universe could be accounted for as the motion of inert objects interacting according to exact laws. Up until fifty years ago the expectation in physics was that this belief would apply all the way down to the ultimate constituents of matter, be they atoms or whatever.

Later

> the discovery that atoms could be divided into more elementary constituents was a triumph of rationality. . . . The billiard ball hypothesis was apparently confirmed. . . . But then, from an unexpected quarter came a shattering blow

when quantum physics asked

> how are you going to *see* these small particles? . . . for the presumption of predictability to be carried out, it is necessary *to observe* the position and momentum.

This proved to be impossible. The observation of position could not be carried out. The position and momentum of particles were indeterminate.

It seemed that for a long time the staunch traditionalist hoped that some finer probe might be made that would contradict this. Young explained that many scientists felt the same, for one does not like to give up one's faith that the universe can be known, or in some other words, that it is *objective*. But, as Heisenberg was at pains to point out, we are up against not merely the physical limitation of an instrument which a better instrument might circumvent. We encounter here a principle which imposes a theoretical limit on the accuracy of our knowledge about individual particles.

For however we vary our probe, the uncertainty is the same; we can measure position with accuracy only at the expense of disturbing the momentum, and we can measure momentum only at the expense of disturbing the position; the product of the two uncertainties is a constant.

Implicit in this dilemma is an important philosophical principle: the observer can know the universe only by interacting with it, and this interaction requires more energy as the accuracy of observation increases. A remarkable finding, for it makes zero as unattainable as infinity!

And this turning point of science had

a moral: the world of fundamental particles is quite different from that of predictable billiard balls. From the point of view of predictability, it is like that of human beings. Its creatures have a life of their own. Predictability here is similar to that of insurance tables, Gallup polls, and market surveys: it does not apply to *individuals*. The individual particle does not obey laws.

The effects of uncertainty on determinism had to be carefully considered, because the Uncertainty Principle applied only to levels of subatomic particles. What was significant, however, was the degree to which uncertainty restored the importance, and consequently the freedom, of the observer. About this freedom Huston Smith wrote,

> If it strikes the reader as presumptuous to equate his personal center with the center of the cosmos, he must be reminded that physics requires him to do just that; because space is relative and curved, the center of the physical universe is for each observer the point from which his observations proceed.

Uncertainty corrected a tendency initiated by Galileo when he effectively separated the observer from the observed. His theory and others that followed created a "primacy of matter" by insisting that the primary qualities of reality were objective measurables, a discovery that led science to a somewhat myopic single vision and the ultimate grief of reductionism. Science made a religion out of reduction. It reduced, tabulated, subdivided, and classified, because it came to believe in the infallibility of measure— the implication that you could reduce everything to matter: the human being, mystery, and even sanctity. But when the infallibility of subatomic measure was successfully challenged by uncertainty, the fatal flaw of reductionism was revealed. In *Where the Wasteland Ends,* Theodore Roszak explained that reductionism was brought on by an arrogant desire to dominate

> from the hasty effort to find simple, comprehensive explanation. In effect . . . to turn whatever is alive into a mere thing.

Acknowledging there was much in science free from re-ductionistic intent, Roszak warned that reductionism was still too much a part of the mainstream of science.

> If the scientific community still can find no way to ex-ile this degrading nonsense from the profession (if, in-deed, it shows no special interest in doing so except at the dissenting fringe) this is for one very definite rea-son. *In principle, there is no way for science to do so without seeming to violate its own most basic values.* Reductionism is quite simply inseparable from single vision. It is born from the act of objectification; it is implied by the assumption that knowledge must be the power to pre-dict and control; it is embedded in the unfortunate no-tion knowledge is to be sought for its *own* sake—as a thing apart from compassion, humanity, wisdom, beauty.

PART TWO

RECOGNITIONS

Some moralist or mythological poet
Compares the solitary soul to a swan;
I am satisfied with that.

                                    —*Yeats*

The time had come to review ruptured wonder and infected seasons more carefully. I seemed to have circled
some edge of understanding from where it seemed possible
to reduce confusion, but in doing this, I was continually
drawn back to the quartets.

   That individual realities of mind/body/spirit/environ-
ment were provinces of psychology/medicine/religion/
science—and manifested in conduct/health/faith/ecol-
ogy—was enlightening but limited. And that schisms existed within each discipline and had far-reaching effects
upon individual well-being was obvious enough. The
problem was what I—or any concerned individual—could
do about the consequences. In order to deal with this problem, it was necessary to understand how a dated dependency on determinism perpetrated a kind of enormous
technological necessity that dominated modern life. Like
countless others I often felt as if I had been vacuumed up
by that necessity. I knew it was simplistic to condemn science for technological ills; on the other hand, without some

analysis of scientific influence, there seemed to be no way to achieve proper perspective of individual well-being. Without some kind of personal empiricism, I feared I well might live out my life subservient to the technological domination science seemed to produce. I was quite willing to applaud the fact that for several hundred years scientific authority had harnessed energy and created the miraculous productivity, communication, and transportation that had so improved existence, but in the second half of my life this progress fed on an exaggerated need for growth that had begun to exhaust the very resources of the Earth. The result was not only pollution and technological disaster like the failure of the Three Mile Island nuclear facility in Pennsylvania—an ecological as well as an outrageous economic failure—but the shocking awareness that the possibility of such catastrophe was often excused as the price of progress.

Early one morning, as I was writing in my journal, Crow stopped by and asked what I was doing. I said I was dismissing science; I was preparing its obituary.

"Well, these are those kinds of times. But don't you think that's extreme? You might dismiss science, but will science be dismissed?"

"From my life? Why not? I've got thirty, perhaps forty, more years to live, and I don't intend spending it dutifully hoping modern science will detoxify itself!"

I aired the old complaint: because a new scientific paradigm might take decades to be accepted, it might not arrive in time to save the world from extinction, much less the American Dream as I knew it. Perhaps this was pompous, perhaps modern calamity was not the failure of science but of the way technology had been utilized. It did not seem to matter. Times were so ugly and unreal, I could no longer tolerate the argument that scientific shortcomings were secondary and, in time, would be rectified. It was time for greater change. Dismissing science was only a symbolic act; still, symbols have always been powerful. Nevertheless, later the same day, it seemed wise to go back and examine each of the schisms again.

The schism in psychology was the most interesting because, years before a New Age had been proclaimed, I had had ample opportunity to observe how a growing interest in humanism had a dramatic effect on behaviorism. In the 1950s Northern California became a platform for those who had begun to challenge traditional puritanism and its adopted twins, Freudianism and behaviorism. The San Francisco Bay Area became a gathering point for people such as Alan Watts, a misanthrope who had left the Episcopal ministry to explore spiritual alternatives such as "active Zen." Watts helped inspire a range of critical inquiry that assured a platform for transactional analysis, transpersonal psychology, est, and, prior to that, institutions such as Synanon and Esalen in Big Sur. These latter two organizations became models for countless growth centers throughout the country. Esalen was especially outstanding, encouraging all kinds of investigation that dealt with creative synthesis and centeredness in the now. Foremost among these inquiries was gestalt therapy, an approach developed by the German-born Fritz Perls, in those days a flamboyant figure even in Big Sur. It was Perls (a protégé of Wilhelm Reich) who inspired all who would listen to "lose your mind and come to your senses!" Long before

Fritz Perls, however, developments in psychology had not only prescribed the humanistic future but successfully questioned the supremacy of Freudianism.

In discussing these developments in psychology, Antoinette Gattozzi explained to the publishing association that although Freudianism and behaviorism had little in common, they shared

> the same mechanistic and dismal outlook on human nature, an outlook in which the human being was basically a mechanism, admirably intricate and marvelously dynamic yet frequently troubled by pathologies of form and content.

According to Gattozzi, in order to deal with these pathologies, it had been important to know the

> design of the machine, that is the human body, brain and nervous system and, once learning its program, probing the patient's memory was the first step to treating pathologies.

Behaviorists concentrated on the design. They were the engineers of the psyche, whereas Freudian psychodynamics focused more on programming and memory. Both were stalkers of the unconscious, but both were concerned

> almost exclusively with pathology and abnormality. Neither had anything positive to contribute to the subject of health and self-generated impulses toward well-being.

Their most unfortunate oversight, however, was their failure to recognize the role of volition, or free will. This blinded them to the potential of human nature and to the self-healing powers of intuition, imagination, and visualization, which they virtually ignored. The universal urge toward transcendence was dismissed as romantic fiction. Gattozzi traced how, despite such shortcomings, these two schools had long dominated modern psychology until the work of

> the eminent psychologist Abraham Maslow. . . . broke their hold. In a series of papers and books spanning the two decades preceding his death in 1970, Maslow led the development of an orientation emphasizing the human potential for self-actualization, creative growth, and joyful living. Humanistic psychology became known as Third Force Psychology, and Maslow recognized that, in its widest meaning, it represented a new worldview. He wrote " . . . it is a Zeitgeist, a spirit of the age, a change of basic thinking along the total front of man's endeavours, a potential change in every social institution, in every one of the 'fields' of intellectual endeavour and in every one of the professions."

Much had changed in the world of therapy since then. By the 1980s there was a dramatic drop in the number of medical students who chose psychiatry. The trend was toward general practice. In 1981 there were more psychiatrists *from* India practicing in America than there were psychiatrists practicing *in* India. Of course Crow wondered how many in India were humanists and how many were behaviorists, but I was not concerned with that. Privately I often wondered why I had never entered psychoanalysis or any kind of formal therapy. This question led to the admission that therapy, especially psychoanalysis, had been an experience I had consciously avoided. It always seemed to be a kind of defeat, a relinquishing of the advantage of discovery. In the 1950s I had known too many who suffered from a kind of dry, fruitless suspension that Freudian analysis seemed to produce; an almost anguished procrastination and indecisiveness, an endless identity-sorting that seared the seasons and allowed precious passage to slip by, never to be recaptured. I had been content to hide in the world of books in order to weather an age of anxiety; satisfied to exalt over the victories of Constance Chatterly and Leopold Bloom while remaining subversively idiosyncratic, a more or less hesitant nihilist. Years later, when the fascination with Freud began to give way to interest in the work of Carl Jung and Joseph Campbell, I came to see that not until humanistic psychology was formalized would it be possible for anyone to question Freudianism, understand the idiosyncratic advantage, or even celebrate the sensual self.

Reviewing the schism in psychology, I became fascinated by behaviorism's dogged dependency on deterministic physics and discovered that many had warned of such dependency. Arthur Young recalled that in 1956 the Nobel Prize physicist Robert Oppenheimer wrote that

> the worst of all possible misunderstandings would occur if psychology should be influenced to model itself after a physics which is not there anymore, which has become outdated.

And writing in the *Saturday Review* in December of 1966, the historian Barbara Tuchman noted

> Let us beware of the plight of our colleagues, the behavioral scientists, who by use of a proliferating jar-

gon have painted themselves into a corner—or isolation ward—of unintelligibility. *They* know what they mean, but no one else does. Psychologists and sociologists are farthest gone in the disease and probably incurable. Their condition might be pitied if one did not suspect it was deliberate. Their retreat into the arcane is meant to set them apart from the great unlearned, to mark their possession of some unshared, unsharable expertise. No matter how illuminating their discoveries, if the behavioral scientists write only to be understood by one another, they must come to the end of the Mandarins.

Yet this was precisely what occurred, and the negative effect of behaviorism on the popular understanding of conduct was devastating, although hardly considered so by behaviorists who, armed with deterministic authority, justified such influence.

Theodore Roszak pointed out the logical continuity that connected the behaviorist's search for a "technology of behavior" with the single vision of the natural sciences. Roszak reminded us that it was B. F. Skinner, American's most influential behaviorist, who, rejecting the unobservable, wrote:

> Physics did not advance by looking more closely at the jubilance of a falling body, or biology by looking at the nature of vital spirits, and we do not need to try to discover what personalities, states of mind, feelings, traits of character, plans, purposes, intentions, or the autonomous man really are in order to get on with a scientific analysis of behavior.

Yet on they went, despite the fact that the closer physicists looked, the less certainty they found.

Young charged it was not science, but scientism—the theory that the methods of investigation used in natural sciences should be applied to all inquiry—that clung to the old determinism; he maintained that science had long been aware of the fact that determinism as a doctrine was untenable. Science, he said, no longer slept what William Blake called Newton's sleep. It was only

> the behaviorist, the sociologist, who "any day now" will discover the "laws" of human behavior. The layman too has endorsed the credo of determinism, perhaps because he feels it is scientific, but also because it gives him security, it exorcises the demons of change.

The question then was, Why, if this had been recognized as early as 1956, behaviorism was able to remain so influential? Crow believed it was because behaviorism so reinforced material belief systems. "Behaviorism isn't limited to the study of rats, my friend! The object of the social scientist is determined control over the human animal. This has great appeal for the materialists—those who *own*. But to achieve this control, the implications of uncertainty and the idea of free will have to be ignored. With freedom and uncertainty, individuals have purpose. They're not on a par with the caged rat or wired-up monkey!"

He was as prejudiced as I was.

"And for good reason! I refuse to consign the fate of the human being to scientism. Uncertainty and the freedom it restores is as much the province of philosophy and religion as science."

"Then why did you think my obituary was an extreme measure?"

He smiled, ignoring the question, yet the next day, artfully pointed out the importance of the brain/mind issue. It proved to be another key area of understanding.

Simply seen, the question was whether the mind was separate from the brain—an enigma for many reasons. The terms *brain* and *mind* had been so flagrantly interchanged that the difference between them was obscured. Even humanists were sometimes confused. But for the behaviorist, or the neurobiologist who joined the fray in the 1970s, there was no difference—mind and brain were one and the same. Behaviorists dismissed speculation that the mind might be independent of the brain or the body, and it was easy to see why. Casual review of the issue brought to light the paramount question that behaviorists refused to consider. If the mind was outside or separate from the brain, it was possibly beyond observable physiology, and perhaps even connected with a Jungian collective unconscious.

Behaviorists said this was impossible. They claimed no *scientific* evidence supported such speculation, and maintained that consciousness, if it did exist, was, like mind, merely a by-product of the brain. Nevertheless, a great deal of ancient and modern evidence supported the theory that the mind was independent of—or at least not totally synonymous with—the brain. The ploy of behaviorists was to fall back on strict determinism, reject evidence that was not "scientific." If something (such as mind) could not be measured, it could not be scientifically considered, and thus the authority of behaviorism was ensured by a kind of self-isolating tautology. But when uncertainty philosophically shattered strict determinism by proving the limitations of measure, the freedom to explore such separation was not only justified, but raised exciting considerations that had been long ignored.

An overview of all of this began with the brain, the amazing brain. It weighed only three pounds, yet used nearly three-quarters of the body's oxygen. Being the body's computer, it was believed to store the memories of a lifetime. But no two brains were alike, though each was divided into left and right hemispheres. The left hemisphere controlled the right side of the body, while the right controlled the left. For many years it had been believed that the left hemisphere handled information and language and was, in a sense, masculine, analytical, and primarily concerned with verbal and mathematical abstractions; whereas the right hemisphere was seen as more feminine, intuitive, and capable of simultaneously processing information in a diffuse way. When modern research corrected earlier belief that the right hemisphere was subordinate to the left, it became clear that each hemisphere made unique contributions to psychological function. Further research into the chemistry of the brain found that it produced more than thirty secretions, which had unique, powerful effects on the body. Still, too little was known.

It was a mystery, for example, why the brain lacked the power to understand itself, why the human being dreamed, or exactly what occurred during hypnosis. When the research of Jerre Levi and others at the University of Chicago suggested that distinct structural differences in male and female brains accounted for different processing, the definition of male and female hemispheres was upset. This posed problems for behaviorists, but there were others. Neurobiologists had never discovered which hemisphere controlled memory. Also, thought could never be attributed to one hemisphere or the other, because both showed activity at all times. In *Toward a Science of Con-*

sciousness, Kenneth Pelletier maintained that no distinction between hemispheres could be considered rigid or dualistic, even though there had been

> an increasing tendency toward an overly simplistic model of the left–right duality of human consciousness by laymen and researchers alike. Despite the popular clichés, the data on hemispheric asymmetry ultimately lends more support to a unitary than to a dualistic view of consciousness.

It took considerable time and patience for the concerned individual, outside the ken of psychology and medicine, to fully appreciate this. Though endlessly fascinating and easily discussed, it was not easily incorporated in an individual sense of things.

There was always more to learn.

In *Beyond Biofeedback,* Elmer and Alyce Green explored the power of the mind to control the body and its unconscious functions, emotions, and states of consciousness. They offered the hypothesis that mind was an energy structure that *included* the brain; they also explained how, according to Patanjali's *Yoga Sutras,* both mind and brain— or body—were seen as "substances, energy structures; the body was merely the densest section of mind." This idea had been summarized a few years before at the Menninger Foundation by the Swami Rama, who claimed that all of the body was in the mind, but not all of the mind was in the body.

As my inquiry progressed, I discovered curious signs of skepticism within the confines of strict science. Surveying the 1920s, the social historian Alan Jenkins remembered that Sir Arthur Eddington, reflecting on the question of whether nature was mechanical or had *mind* behind it, acknowledged that nature might be abstract mathematics, but, Eddington warned, there is "something in human experience that cannot be accounted for by scientific symbolism because it belongs to another world."

Toward a Science of Consciousness shed particular light on this. In the book Pelletier laid groundwork for the integration of philosophy, psychology, neurology, and even religion into the study of consciousness, and in doing so touched on the work of the famous Canadian neurosurgeon Wilder Penfield, the pioneer whose efforts led to the understanding of the electricity of the brain. Late in his life Penfield came to see how, after years of striving to explain the mind on the basis of brain action alone, it was simpler "and far easier . . . if one adopts the hypothesis . . . that . . . it will always be quite impossible to explain the mind on the basis of neuronal action within the brain." Penfield was convinced that the brain was not the organ that produced thought, but an instrument *used* by thought for its own ends. In a prestigious career he had demonstrated in surgery how the mind could use a damaged brain for its own purposes, even though the brain circuitry, normally needed to those ends, had been destroyed. Penfield was not alone in such speculations. The Nobel Prize neurologist John C. Eccles maintained that mind was not reducible to the function of the brain and, in Indiana, the zoologist Paul Pietsch drew other, fascinating conclusions.

Pietsch worked with the salamanders, the favorite animal of the alchemists, who, in medieval times, discovered the animal's amazing regenerative powers. Whenever a leg of the salamander was amputated, the lost limb grew back in a matter of days. Seeking further insight into the mystery of the mind, Pietsch experimented with the brains of salamanders. After countless operations in which brains were removed, mixed, and then replaced, it became obvious that surgical distortion and random replacement did *not* scramble the meaning of information stored in the brain; indeed, if only a portion of brain was replaced, memory was preserved.

This fascinated Crow. For several months he studied and speculated that if certain salamanders were taught to find their way out of a maze, their brains might be removed, scrambled, and then implanted in other salamanders who had no familiarity with the maze. After acquiring brains of their more educated kin, these salamanders might well go through the maze with relatively little difficulty, thus lending oblique support to the idea of the collective unconscious or a *continuum of consciousness* through which knowledge and wisdom were transmitted.

The idea was greatly elaborated on by Rupert Sheldrake, a British plant physiologist from Cambridge. His 1983 book, *A New Science of Life,* caused such a sensation that the prestigious British science magazine *Nature* found it suitable for "burning." Sheldrake theorized that once various organisms learned a task, they could communicate that knowledge to others, independent of distance or time. Sheldrake maintained such transmission was due to a "morphogenetic field."

Months later, while visiting Kenneth Pelletier and reflecting on the continuum of consciousness, he stated that proof of the theory that consciousness was more than brain electricity would emerge only from a revolutionary understanding of purpose and free will. "Until then it's probably best to see that mind—or consciousness—is to the body what time is to the clock."

It seems quite dull and stupid for life to go on the common way.

　　　　　　　　　　　—*Alice in Wonderland*

The schism in medicine—between pathology and prevention—was more complicated, though valuable comparison could still be made. It was equally important to recognize how, by often dwelling on the symptoms of distress and not the cause, traditional pathology failed to recognize the extent to which optimum health resulted from environmental and emotional balance, rather than dependency on surgical or pharmaceutical intervention. Interest in this issue came about at a time when many were discovering that traditional pathology not only conflicted with concepts of prevention but was, in many ways, inconsistent with the aims of human potential. Some were suspicious that traditional pathology was waging an undeclared war on the rising interest in preventive or holistic medicine in order to guard its lucrative domination of health care.

Even if no "medicine war" existed, it could not be denied that traditional medicine indulged in a dependency on drugs and technology. The dependency was not only questionable, but the economic consequences were outrageous and the cultural effects disgraceful. Some observers claimed that the battle lines of a medicine war had been drawn by a closed coalition of vested interests—physicians, pharmaceutical executives, hospital administrators, research institutions, and charity organizations—who aggressively attacked any insinuation that anything was fundamentally wrong with the traditional approach, or that the cost of health care was not justified. On the other side, critics claimed pathology was a twentieth-century hydra incapable of dealing with modern afflictions, and there was much evidence to support the claim. By 1980 America led the world in per capita health expenditure, yet in several other countries, health care not only cost less but was considered superior. Nationwide surveys revealed that the most common consumer complaint was against the medical profession, probably because the cost of health care had risen more than 200 percent over a period of time when the national consumer index had risen only 87 percent. Also, in geographical areas where the number of physicians had increased, the cost of medical services had actually risen.

These amounted to only a casual selection of complaints. More shocking problems hid in the background. In October 1980 the American Medical Association was urged by Arnold Relman, M. D., then editor of the prestigious *New England Journal of Medicine,* to declare it unethical for physicians to receive income derived from health care, except for fees for services. His call was in response to the accusation that doctors were creating conflicts of interest by ownership of for-profit hospitals, nursing homes, laboratory services, and clinics. Relman warned that the medical profession risked losing the confidence of the public.

Scholarly study further dimmed the glitter of the modern medical miracle. There was evidence that improvements in sanitation, shelter, farming, food processing, and transportation had had far greater effect on health and the quality of twentieth-century life than had advances in medicine. The most incisive minds asked, Why, when modern America was relatively free of plague and pestilence, were modern afflictions—cancer, heart attack, stroke, and depression—so rampant?

To me the idea of a medicine war was questionable, but to highlight this ongoing hyperbole, Crow would periodically announce results of the battle between the forces of surgical/pharmaceutical intervention and those of humanistic alternatives. Reporting into an imaginary microphone, he would declare that "Sloan-Kettering today revealed that its synthetic surgery strike force destroyed a macrobiotic diet commune in Lyme, New Hampshire!" Or he would demand that cancer, "the most murderous of the modern afflictions," be designated a national plague in order to alert concerned individuals to "the real reality!" He once distributed a memo to the publishing associates comparing the ravages of cancer with imaginary rats streaming out of polluted environments to gnaw on the entrails of an unsuspecting public. As ghoulish as it seemed, the metaphor was not inaccurate. In 1982 statistics showed that, contrary to the impression given by the American Cancer Society, the war on cancer, announced by President Nixon in 1972, was hardly successful. In 1986 a report from the Harvard School of Public Health suggested that the technological efforts of radiation and chemotherapy were, for the most part, a failure. On another occasion Crow, always the avid associate, brought in a fundraising poster from the American Cancer Society that read, "Please don't quit on us now. We're halfway there!"

He exclaimed, "Jesus! I ask you! This from an institution that in 1978 spent less than 6 percent of its income on assistance to individual patients, yet $10,000 a day on the telephone?" When it was pointed out that statistics could be deceptive and that he was quoting 1978 figures in 1982, he came back a week later, armed with 1982 figures challenging the society's explanation that cancer, being a disease of old age, only appeared to be on the rise because, in modern times, people lived longer.

"This doesn't explain the shocking increase in cancer among children or the sorry focus on chemotherapy and radiation that ignores the horrendous side effects!" Radiation drew his particular scorn, especially the CAT scanner, a computer axial tomography machine in which the whole patient was inserted for X-ray diagnosis. "If you don't have cancer when you go in that rocket," he warned, "you'll sure as hell have it by the time you come out the other end!"

Months later I told him I thought his whole approach was unwise, perhaps unfair, because some surgical and pharmaceutical interventions did work, and whatever might bring relief should be encouraged. It was my contention that once an individual's body disintegrated or decayed to a certain point, cancer could begin. And any holistic effort to correct psychophysiological well-being was thin defense at that point, leaving drugs or therapy as the only alternative.

"You might be right, but economically it's still a war. But I admire your idealism, Briggs. I more than admire it—I envy it."

The medical establishment did not react kindly to alternatives or criticism. Criticism from within was dismissed as an unfortunate myopia of malcontents and from without was made to seem unfounded or misinformed. Official reaction usually ended in lofty admonishment about the need for confidence in scientific procedure and faith in further expenditure. About that time attacks on holistic medicine had become more pronounced; and in the *New England Journal of Medicine,* almost irrational. In April 1983, suspending its usual tempered editorial stance, the journal carried an article by Doctors Glymour and Stalker in which the practice of medicine was seen as a "form of consultant engineering" in which "there were people rather than bridges." Holistic medicine was described as "a pablum of common sense and nonsense offered by cranks and quacks and failed pedants who shared an attachment to magic and an animosity toward reason."

In light of all this, the so-called medicine war seemed an ideal subject for a book, but nothing ever came of the idea. Once, when the possibility was discussed, one associate extended the metaphor when he asked whether a medicine war turned the concerned individual into a "hapless refugee." The comment was made in the middle of an editorial meeting in which everyone present was well aware of the problem and tried to see it in a large and sober context. In reply to Crow's accusation that the cost of health care was criminal, the point was made that costs were relative. Few Americans were particularly aware of the benefits of preventive medicine. The fact was that—at the time—overweight, overworked, and almost impervious to warnings about diet and consumption, Americans were making more than a billion visits a year to physicians. Disregarding the rage of fitness that was sweeping select segments of society, the general public, that amorphously mediaed mass, was getting the kind of health care it deserved. When Crow took exception to the public being considered an amorphously mediaed mass, he was cleverly questioned about his claim that the cost of health care was criminal.

What were his facts?

He cited a 1978 congressional study that put the cost of unnecessary surgery at $4 billion and 10,000 unnecessary deaths, and he referred to a study from Indiana University and the University of Western Ontario that was critical of stroke surgery. The approximately 108,000 operations performed annually cost more than $1.2 billion and failed to benefit patients in three out of four cases. Another congressional study revealed that in 1976 physicians wrote 27 million prescriptions for sleeping pills—a billion doses—responsible for 25,000 emergency treatments and 5000 deaths.

Listening to this, I realized how much our editorial meetings had changed in ten years. I had long ago moved from Cow Hollow and, after setting up offices in Berkeley and then Point Richmond, settled in Marin County, just north of San Francisco. Only two of the original associates remained. Nevertheless, the quality and range of interest had broadened. Opinion was more informed and disagreement more easily weathered, but trade publishing was as unpredictable as ever, and a few lucrative months were usually required to sustain several lean years.

At the time business considerations seemed secondary to the questionable application of New Age fundamentals that was taking place, especially in healing. Disturbing situations could be found among those who had taken amateurish interest in healing and begun experimenting with a variety of methods from acupressure to psychic healing, from the generalized use of energy to the laying on of hands. There were few sound models. Among self-appointed healers there was often only vague and naive understanding of the ramifications of distress and little awareness of the healer's responsibilities, one of which was to protect against harmful side effects.

Traditional healers never ignored this kind of protection. Just as the surgeon wore gloves and a mask or the X-ray technician a lead shield, so the experienced traditional or native healer employed various means to neutralize reactions that could afflict anyone within the radius of a healing ceremony. On one occasion in 1973, when I accompanied Rolling Thunder to a healing, the medicine man covered our faces, shoulders, and arms with a yellow cornmeal paste to protect us from "the trouble" he anticipated that day. After witnessing a four-hour ceremony, an exorcism of a debilitating possession, it was apparent the precautions afforded an indefinable security. I felt the effects but never asked about the contents of the paste, knowing I would never have been told.

In the years that followed this incident, I was able to draw other conclusions from scattered but vivid observations and impressions. Protection was not the primary concern. The primary concern seemed to be to know when *not* to heal. Lack of traditional training or foolish exhibitionism sometimes led amateurs to attempt to relieve any distress whatsoever; by doing so, they unwittingly sided with pathologists, who typically treated all symptoms regardless of the cause. They imitated incantation or the laying on of hands or mixed varieties of massage with attempts to induce, channel, or control energy, but few self-appointed healers understood that traditional healers believed that, under certain conditions, distress should not be relieved, because it might be part of a necessary or natural process or experience. Although sympathetic and responsive to suffering, native healers also recognized that the origin of a distress could originate outside the present life of the body, and they were prepared to deal with the consequences of this. Except when distress was induced by evil or negative influence from outside a victim's ordinary reality, native healers tried to divert distress or cause it to disintegrate through exposure, rather than try to heal it.

It was always important to ascertain when a source of distress might be originating outside the body or environment, and this often led to overwhelming questions. If distress was having a negative effect upon an individual's way of life, should it be allowed to continue or should attempts be made to alleviate it? If experiencing distress was necessary for recovery, should the range of distress be allowed to include death? The answer of the native healer was yes, but this could set off all kinds of alarm in those not of the healer's tradition.

The sympathy of native healers was as perplexing as their methods. Some American Indian medicine people were known to wait three days before deciding whether to treat a victim; during that time the victim was presumed to be safe while the medicine person prayed or searched for signs of the trouble, or decided upon means or herbs that might be used to relieve the suffering. Relief was always the paramount concern, but the extent to which the distress might have originated out of interaction with other lives or spirits could be equally as important. In some cases distress was never completely relieved, so that the victim could become aware of its origins or reasons, but this was unusual.

I once heard a story about how Rolling Thunder helped the victim of an automobile accident who was in a coma and not responding to treatment in the hospital. He visited the victim and performed a hurried ceremony at the bedside. There, using his eagle feather, he went into a trance in which he returned to the scene of the accident, found the spirit—which had been separated from the body by the shock of the crash—and guided the spirit back to the body. Within minutes the victim came out of the coma and ultimately recovered. Questioned about this incident, Rolling Thunder was evasive, claiming only that medicine people rarely moved a shock victim until they were certain that the victim's spirit was present. The inference was that in rushing a victim away from an accident, all that might be accomplished would be the removal of a body that was doomed without its spirit.

While diagnosing distress some native healers were known to "read into" the life of a patient, perhaps through the patient's aura, but readings like these were always delicate. The more powerful the healer, the more circumspect the interpretation, because distress might be only a small stain in a vast symmetry such a reading could reveal. A reading might enlighten, but only if a victim was capable of seeing beyond the experience in which the reading occurred. Even though most native healers were spiritually enlightened, enlightenment did not seem to be their primary concern. Care had to be exercised. The failure to separate healing and enlightenment ran the risk of leading a patient beyond levels of familiar understanding. Not that the native healer would refuse to enlighten; it was rather that healing seemed to depend upon a particular respect for the difference between healing and enlightenment. This led some to believe that the more powerful the healer, the less she or he would attempt any radical or collective correction. The healing of groups or geographical areas was usually avoided; most healers remained within a conservative purity of practice.

Healers were put off by inquiry which tried to determine a correlation between the life they led and the powers available to them. Power was never used for gain. Talented healers were indifferent to reward or recognition by authority, and artfully remained anonymous out of respect for forces that could be attracted to healing and the material politics that often surrounded its influence. It seemed that most healers found it wise to be indifferent; they might even be poor at handling money or somewhat bored by the popular excitement surrounding the New Age interests. They were careful never to violate some *other* fundamental harmony which was known to be tenuous and always in flux. To step outside the natural rhythms of this and accept a mundane challenge to their talent invited reaction that could upset even a gifted shaman. This made indifference a wise design and punctured the image of the supershaman or all-knowing don who would reveal the secrets of other worlds, a myth self-appointed healers loved to embellish.

Such fiction fascinated some New Age circles, but it ignored a larger universal orientation and overlooked the fact that in most traditions healers were not self-appointed. Often recognized at birth, they were subjected to years of practice in order to understand the difference between learning and knowing. Knowing was the product of endless learning and involved travel so intricate that the journeys made fictional marvels insipid.

I became aware of this during one of my trips to New York. After a few days of business in Manhattan and dinner with my father in New Jersey, I made arrangements to continue on to Buffalo, New York, to visit Mad Bear, a Tuscarora medicine man I had met several times in California. I had finally remarried and that freedom, which at one time I might have considered a restraint, allowed me to cross other borders I had previously ignored. The object of the visit to Buffalo was to renew a friendship and to inquire about a curious affair that had long fascinated me.

Mad Bear, whose Americanized name was Wallace Anderson, was born and raised near Buffalo, and in 1978 still lived on the Tuscarora reservation. Located near Niagara Falls, the reservation had that particularly ambiguous atmosphere of oppression that lingers over most Indian reservations. Famous as a healer, Mad Bear was also well known for his role in communicating the values of traditional American Indians.

Mad Bear's road had never been an easy one. As a boy he had been introduced to Indian medicine because most of his elders still lived in the traditional way; his favorite grandmother was well versed in the secrets of healing. Federal law required he attend La Salle High School in Buffalo, but a youthful desire to escape led him to spend nearly twenty years at sea, travel that offered opportunities to explore and compare healing in many parts of the world. Drawn back to the reservation several times, he was eventually apprenticed to Eleazor Williams, a Tuscarora healer, and, after Eleazor Williams died, was befriended by Peter Mitten, a Cayuga medicine man of great reputation. He worked with Peter Mitten for years, and the two of them made many trips across the United States, healing and appealing for restoration of traditional values among Indians of every tribe. It was during one of these trips that they became involved in the aforementioned curious affair.

On the West Coast in June 1970, the two medicine men were summoned to San Francisco General Hospital by Anne Oaks, the wife of a young Indian activist who had played a prominent part in the sensational civil rights occupation of the deserted federal prison on Alcatraz Island. Richard Oaks had suffered a severe concussion in a fight in the San Francisco Mission District and was in intensive care; when he did not respond to conventional medical treatment, his wife insisted that Indian medicine people be allowed to attend him. Only because of the sensitive political climate of the time was this request even considered, and only after pitiless bureaucratic procrastination. Mad Bear and Peter Mitten were delayed by hours of pointless negotiations between civil rights lawyers and hospital authorities who wanted to know the treatment and medicines that were to be used, information they were repeatedly told could not be revealed. The hospital authorities also insisted that a potentially incriminating release be signed by the medicine men, who, in point of fact, were forbidden by state law from practicing medicine, let alone in a public hospital. The hospital, of course, was in a difficult position. The staff physicians and administrators who were treating Oaks had privately agreed that he had little chance to survive—his skull had been cruelly fractured—yet they were under popular political pressure to share his care with the medicine men. If the medicine men were brought in and Oaks died, they could be open to charges of negligence; on the other hand, if he lived, it would be claimed that red medicine worked where white failed.

After prolonged argument, in which the medicine men reluctantly (or deceptively) admitted that they would be using herbs to cure Oaks, the authorities were pressed to relent. Agitated by the cruel delay, Peter Mitten, an unusually taciturn man, took Mad Bear aside and said the situation was too grave for more talk and recommended that they sign the hospital's release because it was only "white paper." Within minutes the release was executed, the medicine men acted, and—to the amazement of hospital authorities—Richard Oaks recovered.

All kinds of secondhand stories came out of this incident, because press coverage of the event had been spotty and incomplete. When it was over hospital spokespeople were able to dismiss the importance of the medicine men, for the simple reason that once the Indians had treated Oaks they left immediately. The *San Francisco Chronicle* was told that in the eyes of the medical staff the medicine men were religious figures whose services were considered religious rites, and it had been felt that "herbs would not hurt the patient."

Never responsibly investigated, the incident became hopelessly obscured. Years later there was no way for anyone to confirm the story that, as the medicine men began to work over Richard Oaks, a hospital observer saw a white bird circling over the bed, a device known to keep the spirit from leaving the body. Later the observer bitterly recanted the observation, refused to discuss the matter with anyone, and subsequently disappeared in retirement.

My meeting with Mad Bear was memorable, but it was not until a month later in California that I fully appreciated the subtlety of his character. Whether discussing complexities of purification or the simple need to give daily thanks to food, not to the god who provided it, Mad Bear's manner was compelling yet always reserved. Once, while discoursing on the history of corn, he talked of the language and music of rain and explained that there were two kinds: a heavy, whippish *male* rain, and a softer, more indirect *female* rain. Occasionally the two might merge, but more often than not they were separate and produced different effects that depended on the place as well as the season or the need of the earth. When we discussed the link between stress and cancer and its connection with health and spirit, he delivered a long, impressive monologue on the disease, wondering whether cancer was actually a spiritual sickness in that its evils disrupted the harmonious balance of the body long before the distress was recognized.

Weeks later, listening to tapes of some of our conversations, the satisfaction of the visit was suddenly ruptured when I realized I had forgotten to ask Mad Bear about the Oaks affair. I did not know when I would see him again and was not only agitated but mystified as to why I had failed to ask about the white bird or about several other aspects of the healing. Slowly, reviewing the tone and mood of the visit, I realized I had not forgotten to ask these questions but had instead *suspended* them in the back of my mind. Another week of perplexing review passed before it occurred to me that perhaps Mad Bear had somehow "induced" the suspension, perhaps to teach me the patience of learning, perhaps to spare me a feeling of rejection because certain revelations would not be made.

Shamans were always artful.

So artful that I came to see a relationship between my

search for change and the depth of traditional Indian re-spect for earth, sky, water, and air—elements that should never be profaned. From that relationship I began to see a grand design, an intricate mandate marred only by the way these primary guardians of Indian traditions were ma-ligned by those who insisted the practice of medicine was a "form of consultant engineering" in which the projects were "people rather than bridges."

let's go then
let's kiss God on the mouth!
                    —*David Meltzer*

A few months later, still circling that edge of understanding from where it seemed possible to reduce my confusion, I went back to Paris. After twenty-three years it was more magnificent than I had remembered it; the boulevards and buildings were astonishing and the midget signatures of the neighborhoods enchanting. André Malraux had cleansed public buildings, and from the Quai Montebello, Notre Dame seemed exquisitely remote. The weather had turned around. The March light was marvelous and, except for haircut and glasses, taxi drivers were no different from those in New York the day before. After an appointment with a French literary agent, I joined my wife and we strolled through the Luxembourg Gardens, where the trees showed early signs of spring above the stains of winter still on the worn sidewalks.

In the Deux Magots little had changed. Faces still hovered over serious ashtrays and conversations were animated. Hours later we decided to walk through the streets until one restaurant seemed inviting enough. The evening ended in another café, where the port was delicious but soiled by the exhaust of passing traffic and the fact that, besides drinking rivers of coffee potted with white sugar, Parisians still smoked incessantly. But these complaints seemed obtuse, almost ridiculous, the espionage of some reformed puritan inhibited by prejudice that did not travel.

The next day the sky was gray. When I lost my way looking for the Pompidou Center, I retired to a small park, where my irritation at the silly failure reminded me for some reason of Mad Bear's reference to cancer as a spiritual sickness that began long before it was recognized. The idea led to thoughts of the schism in religion between dogma and mystery, a consideration that occupied a permanent place on the back of my desk in San Francisco. As the moments wore on, my own spiritual problem inspired a peculiar illumination that seemed to filter through the stalks of the weathered doorways that followed the curbs toward the Seine, a few blocks away.

Early the next morning I left our hotel and wandered down the Rue des Reines until I came upon a small bakery where I bought a baton of bread that was still warm when I returned to the room. My wife made chamomile tea, and near the window I studied the spread of the city below. The spiritual problem rose out of the skyline again. Breaking off a crust of bread, I recalled the glazed donuts I used to enjoy in Omaha forty years before. I was an altar boy then, an idealist who had grown more agnostic every winter since. The parallel between donuts and French bread seemed almost comic, but not in light of the legacy of lost Catholicism that lay bleached and scattered across prairies of neglected wonder, across a landscape now dotted with neglected churches, deserted schools, and impoverished rectories from which so many of the finer priests and nuns had retired. The original simplicity of Jesus had been obscured by centuries of adjusted dogma—original sin, the tragic denial of reincarnation, canon law that made marriage a sacrament and divorce a sin. In *Maps of Consciousness* Ralph Metzner pointed out the primary inconsistency:

> That Jesus taught with light and healed with fire will be evident to anyone who reads the lines of the uncanonical gospels or between the lines of the orthodox gospels. And he taught also that "What I do all men can do. I come to show the possibilities of man." But, as has happened so many times in the past, his teachings were distorted so that men emphasized the worship of *him* as a divine being, rather than the practice of his teaching, which was—for each man to recognize that he is himself a divine being, to seek the kingdom of heaven within, and to bring it forth into manifestation.

From the sill of the hotel window, I reflected that the problem came down to whether spiritual disenchantment could be realistically evaluated between donuts and French bread. Why not? I was American enough to expect revelation in Paris, and before the week was over it had become obvious that the schism between dogma and mystery paralleled the erosion by material determinism of belief in superhuman power. A week later, flying home, this recognition was uncomfortable. Over the ocean and prairies and mountains, I seemed to be floating above an enormous contradiction—a maze in which spiritual renewal was locked in a paradox of empty churches and crowded ashrams that dotted the Earth below.

By 1980 the spiritual problem in America had been exacerbated by a growing interest in Eastern alternatives and further complicated by Western revivalists. The Eastern alternatives, offering freedom from the guilt of original sin and from threats of limbo, purgatory, and hell, glowed with the bone white appeal of enlightenment and bliss and filled a terrible void that, war after war, had grown more intolerable. Yet contemporary as they seemed, Western experiments with Eastern alternatives were not new. As I ate glazed donuts in Omaha in the 1940s, the English expatriates Aldous Huxley and Christopher Isherwood were rising before dawn in Los Angeles to meditate in a Vendanta center before Swami Prabhavananda, a Hindu monk of the Ramakrishna order. In the 1950s the Beat Generation had been deeply influenced by Zen Buddhism, and by 1970 Eastern alternatives had been colorfully paraded by such celebrities as the Beatles. Tibetan Buddhists, whom Crow considered Asian Jesuits, had opened influential institutes in Berkeley and Boulder, Colorado. Hari Krishna groups danced and panhandled on street corners, and zealous young converts, disguised behind smoking incense and four-color pamphlets, hustled money in airports to finance assorted pundits, swamis, and a variety of spiritual centers across the country. The potential of "the God within" had been widely recognized, yet it was not, by any means, accidental transformation. The change had been prophesied. In the eighth century an Eastern master foretold that "when the iron bird flies and horses run on wheels, the Tibetan people will be scattered like ants across the world and the Dharma will come to the land of the Red Man."

The success of Eastern gurus and philosophies in the American void was complicated by the fact that a revival of Christian fundamentalism was taking place at the same time. Although both were coarsely distorted by the media, whether performed for the glory of Jesus, Buddha, or Allah, arrival and revival alike seemed unable to overcome the materialistic determinism in which the concerned individual seemed so imprisoned. Many of the publishing associates felt materialism was a political problem. I disagreed. The malicious persuasiveness of materialism caused spiritual as well as cultural and psychological disorientation, and when the center of worship failed to offer realistic removal—a place where higher need could be rescued from material peril—the material promise became so dazzling that spiritual significance was blurred. When this occurred the dangers of stress, once dismissed as onerous by-product of opportunity and success, became a source of modern affliction, the spiritual sickness about which Mad Bear had cautioned.

In Paris it had been easier to see how matters that affected the mind, body, and environment affected the spirit and soul. Though I was unable to put the religious schism into better perspective in Paris, it was the actualization of perspective that proved most difficult. In the early 1970s, in order to begin a serious evaluation of my separation from Catholicism, I went to great lengths to contact a young priest, a promising theologian whose views on spiritual renewal were reputed to be original and inspiring. The search proved fruitless. In the year or two it took to secure a proper address, I learned that he had left the church, suffered a rash marriage and bitter divorce, and one night had been killed in an automobile accident on Route 80, somewhere south of Gila Bend, Arizona. I tried to learn more, but my sources proved biased or unreliable. One exparishioner, in a rambling fifty-five-minute telephone call, told me that the priest had been killed in New Mexico, not Arizona, and had been driven by a "diabolical urge to destroy the church." I had trouble believing that. Another woman said that with "the advent of feminism he was doomed." When I asked why, she said he was "just too damned attractive to women" and urged me to pray for his soul.

I never did.

The impact of Eastern arrivals was more profound than many observers were willing to admit. They captivated the mature as well as the young, yet despite the enthusiasm that grew out of their activities, disappointments eventually mounted. For many converts the promise began to pale when, along with Western revivals, the Eastern alternative also failed to realistically address Whole Earth needs. The common complaint was that the Eastern alternative was too elaborately confined. The seeker often discovered that the Eastern structure of spiritual inspiration combined with physical technique, which was so impressive at the start, often proved disappointing and polluted by religious and economic politics. Initiation and practice failed to translate into *independent* vision. The enlightenment and wondrous techniques of psychophysiological well-being, developed over thousands of years, were rarely tailored for individual consumption. And the techniques often went hand in hand with a strict philosophy or stricter allegiance to a figurehead. This was immaterial to the few who were chosen, but ultimately intolerable to the many who were called.

Early on I was perplexed why Western revivals did not recognize the holistic appeal of psychophysiological spirituality but, having learned from awkward experience how difficult it could be to utilize yoga and meditation, I had to be realistic. Even with the advantage of having worked with individuals who dealt professionally or passionately with alternatives, it had been difficult to appreciate the link between physical well-being and spiritual renewal, and, were it not for previous experience with other ways and means of altering awareness, I might never have made the connection.

Many were surprised at the spontaneous reception given Eastern alternatives, but they should not have been mystified. In New Age theaters, if any offering was dramatic or sincere enough, it could easily attract indiscriminate attention. This trend created bogus reputations that later had to be carefully appraised. It was odd that compared with religion, credibility was more quickly established in psychology, medicine, and science; there critics and sympathizers alike were able to grasp essentials and, armed with tougher, more rational reference, better able to evaluate and debate ideas. In religion, understanding was more elusive and designs not as easily evaluated. Crow considered this "an unfortunate problem of digestion" in which new concepts in psychology, medicine, and science were "quickly absorbed," but religious considerations were "badly passed." He was quick to point out that although most competent psychologists and scientists were seldom inspiring speakers, their messages were more readily defined; whereas religious leaders, though traditionally more persuasive, often labored with vague or abstract ideas.

Revivals had other problems—not only the failure to deal with physical and material malignancy, but an inability to refute the contemporary supposition that God was dead. In North Beach in the late 1950s, I and many others made the mistake of believing Edmund Wilson when he announced that the word *God* was archaic, and ought to be dropped by those who did not need it for moral support. The death of God gave credibility to the behaviorists' claim that the soul (if it did exist) was only an "accessory" like the mind, simply another area for scientific investigation. At the zenith of the Space Age, with a Spartan astronaut mastering one giant step for mankind, it was difficult to object to such rational appeal. But until the death of God could be scientifically confirmed, a thin misgiving, a dim doubt, a thirst no authority could quench became more noticeable. Concerned individuals began to ask how God could be dead when religious authority did not agree on who or what God was? Or if, because the godhead varied with culture and geography, was every God dead? There seemed to be a flood of spiritual doubt, and in the wake of that the Eastern arrival appeared. He was not in doubt. He believed God was within everyone, even that everyone was God; he believed that enlightenment was infinite and cosmic and could save anyone, anywhere, so long as devotion was total and proper techniques were employed.

To understand the impact such loving conviction had on tight, white American society, it was necessary to acknowledge the accomplishments of these arrivals. It was wrong to be amused by cynically slanted media coverage of flower-strewn scenes in which ardent devotees bobbed and tinkled through hazes of incense to pay homage to bearded, wizened holy men. Shrewder evaluation was required. It was necessary to observe or anonymously linger near a Muktananda or a Tharthang Tulku Rinpoche in order to appreciate the overwhelming presence and the practical control of charisma these men possessed. They

seemed to radiate personal power, and their radiance provided immediate spiritual relief by affirming the belief that
mind was central to true spiritual understanding of existence, which was beyond time, place, and, certainly, materialism. Before such power scientific determinism became inconsequential, and the multifarious miracles of
technology withered. Many spiritually starved Americans,
who could not establish or maintain positive rhythms of
the body or limit their appetites, were overwhelmed. The
arrivals humiliated timid achievers and humbled tor-
mented skeptics. Urging the spiritually dispossessed to
turn from gothic guilt toward the joy of the self and the
soul, arrivals brought miraculous possibilities. Then, carefully exercising the politics of traditional organization,
they created communities and became gurus or babas to
thousands of lost deviants for whom technocracy had become a cretinous hell. Later, by patiently sifting qualifica-
tions of converts and utilizing talents, arrivals were able to
expand their missions beyond anyone's wildest dreams. As
a consequence, tax-freed ashrams and centers secured
property and portfolio that was often protected by legal
and economic expertise—all of which had little to do with
red people but certainly fulfilled prophecy. After a journey
that included a speech before the British parliament and a
visit to Chicago, the Swami Vivekananda, an early arrival,
returned to India in 1897 and declared:

> Once more the world must be conquered by India.
> This is the great ideal before us. Let them come and
> flood the land with their armies, never mind. Up, In-
> dia, and conquer the world with your spirituality!
> Spirituality must conquer the West. Where are the

men ready to go out to every country in the world
with the messages of the great sages of India? There
is no other alternative, we must do it or die. The only
condition of . . . more vigorous national life is the
conquest of the world by Indian thought.

In the startling light of this phenomenon, perspective
was sometimes blurred. Crow was quick to focus loose
impressions. "I read somewhere that in India 350 million
gods are worshiped, so maybe you ought to be careful
about quoting one Munshi!" At the time we were driving
back from a symposium on the spiritual void in America.
One of the speakers spoke eloquently about the difficulties
of searching for spiritual renewal in Western materialism
and of the ironies of the search; a former Catholic, she out-
lined the disintegration of Catholicism and touched upon
the Vatican's connection to the billion-dollar Ambrosiano
bank scandal in the 1970s and the link between financially
powerful television evangelists and right wing political
groups that had been instrumental in the election of Ronald Reagan to the presidency in 1980. But she made no
mention of Eastern arrivals, which was odd, because only
the week before, the Bhagwan Shree Rajneesh, leader of a
world-famous ashram in Poona, India, had been seen on
the television news riding in a two-toned Rolls Royce
through a 75,000-acre Oregon tract that his organization
had recently purchased. Rajneesh had serenely palmed
blessings through closed windows to followers, who had
been dressed in orange and had worn medallions embla-
zoned with his picture. Before I turned north on the 280
freeway south of San Jose, Crow wondered, "Wasn't it Father Divine who said, 'It ain't easy being God'?"

I was not sure.

It was late and we were driving too fast and too high above the spiritual maze. I was unable to see how spiritual renewal could ever take place in a society in which God had been declared dead, media evangelists were millionaires, and a guru owned 75,000 acres of Oregon. Evaluations seemed fruitless.

"You're probably right," Crow agreed. "The last time we tried, we argued about Zen all night." Just below Palo Alto, he wondered whether Zen should be considered a philosophy or a religion.

I still was not sure.

The freeway had become an endless cement strip; we were beyond distinctions. Further discussion seemed immaterial; masters and teachers, pastors and preachers, the farther we traveled, the more they appeared to become threats to the democracy of the soul, antiquated toll collectors whose importance had begun to exceed the gates they guarded. Just south of Golden Gate Park, near the San Francisco Zoo, I remarked on the magnificence of the full moon. Its pearled singularity seemed softer than ever and peculiarly indifferent in the attendant sky, where its huge, round glow mesmerized and assured both of us that the problem of spiritual renewal was due to far more than schisms within disciplines.

The following Sunday, in order to sort out impressions, I set aside several hours to study television evangelists, but they were so insipid that the effort proved fruitless. Out of curiosity I reread Rajneesh's *Book of Secrets*. Published long before his glorious arrival and ignominious departure from the United States, the book was just as impressive on second reading. Rajneesh was one of the most erudite of the arrivals and quoted Lao-tzu and Confucius as easily as Jesus, Emerson, and Gurdjieff. *The Book of Secrets* was not only a sophisticated work, but warm as well. Through the spirit of Buddha, Rajneesh touched the repressed heart and cut through material trouble and the mysteries of sex in order to show how to transcend them. His words were soothing and his ideas engaging, but much like the television evangelist, he never ventured outside the boundaries of his own traditional obedience. He ignored the new. He was a star in what Peter Marin called "the transcendental game of follow the leader," and to heed his call ultimately led to the acceptance of tradition and rejection of the possibility that the trials of an uncertain world might be a process that could lead far beyond circles of obedience.

It was a curious quandary. For more than a decade I had watched some of the finest minds of my generation disappear into fixed circles that led past another blessed toe or rugged cross. I tried not to condemn or condone them, but could not help feeling that such processions were not always spiritually motivated. Some may have been divinely inspired, but too many seemed tortured by an inability to survive in a world in which desires, attachments, and relationships had become the source of unbearable stress.

There was always a rub!

Material absolutism seemed doomed by the freedom of uncertainty. The signs were everywhere, especially in New Age interests and humanistic psychology, holistic medicine, and the politics of ecological awareness. Yet the surest sign was the magnificence of the soft, mysterious moon, which symbolized a new spiritual reorientation emerging out of the rise of female wisdom.

It has long been my conviction that only by the magic of art, or of individuality, can men save themselves. Evil and ugliness are the same thing . . . and dullness is the mother of both. It is not the material conditions of the times so much that darkens the hues of the future, but man's self-satisfaction in the midst of the cataclysms he provokes.

—Osbert Sitwell

The visit with Mad Bear had been a cold crossroad that had revealed the frustrating gap between understanding and action and revived my need for actualization. It was one thing to perceive the effects of humanism on behaviorism—or prevention on pathology, mystery on dogma, uncertainty on determinism—it was quite another matter to transform perception into action. This led back to the quartets.

Originally, a quartet of human realities

mind	body
spirit	environment

had been transposed into a quartet of individual concerns

conduct	health
faith	ecology

the provinces of the four disciplines of

psychology	medicine
religion	science

But when responsibility for conduct, health, faith, and ecology was indiscriminately given over to partisan authority, the concerned individual became subject to a col-

103

lective ambivalence that reduced problems by specializing them. Actualization was then sacrificed to academic considerations. I began to see that in order to correct this, it was imperative that concerned individuals begin to assume greater responsibility for the conduct of their lives, their health, the faith that sustained them, and the ecology of their personal environments.

The wise thing to do was to translate each concern into a separate action over which there was the freedom of personal control. This called for a fifth, or action, quartet. Unlike the previous four, however, the fifth did not simply materialize. In fact, it proved to be ambiguous and elusive. I finally decided that conduct was best related to exercise, or fitness; health to diet, or consumption. Faith was related to meditation, the key to spiritual renewal, and ecology was related to lifestyle.

conduct	health
faith	ecology

or

exercise	diet
meditation	lifestyle

The relationship between conduct and exercise evolved from a conviction that the energy and agility provided by physical fitness not only improved self-confidence but provided the poise with which moments and manners could be more ably managed. Without the benefit of fitness, cognition and even creativity suffered; the lack of energy and agility began to affect the personal style of action and reaction.

The primary factor of health, I believed, was sound diet, not only of what food was consumed but of all visual and sensory input, whatever was taken in through the skin.

The relationship between faith and meditation was less direct. When I considered the problem of stress, I found meditation to be the single most effective antidote. Meditation was physically and psychologically beneficial; it ensured calm order. But experience proved it was impossible to establish a habit of meditation without eventually coming into contact with mystery. Consequently, when I was able to sustain meditation for long periods, I came into contact with an instinctual and usually neglected spiritual longing—a longing that had been lost in the climate that produced the stress. It was peculiar how relief from the worst affliction revived the need for spiritual renewal.

The first three relationships were somewhat obvious, but deciding upon action that would actualize ecology was difficult. Of course a correlation between ecology and lifestyle was vague, but I could not come up with a better alternative. This was unfortunate because it was important that lifestyle (or whatever actualization of ecology was chosen) be seen as a condition that could be individually and internally revised, not merely measured externally or popularly defined. Then what should be the action of lifestyle? If lifestyle "reflected the attitudes and values of an individual or a culture," the action of lifestyle might be a continual reevaluation of every attachment and relationship, and revision of those bonds that influenced where and how an individual lived and why and with whom time was spent.

I was continually warned that the action quartet was too neat, that it hardly addressed larger questions of consciousness. Perhaps so, but nevertheless it did provide a framework in which individual control could begin. What soon became apparent was the importance of *unifying* all four actions in order to create a significant difference. The typical mistake was to become obsessed with either exercise or dietary extremes, meditation, or the endless geometry of lifestyle. Diana Saltoon considered these actions four aspects of awareness and emphasized the necessity of unifying them "in such a way as to experience new security in order to protect and develop the self in the chaos of a polluted, materialistic world." With unification, however, came the need to distinguish between awareness and consciousness. To me, awareness and consciousness were different steps toward knowing, but the terms had become so generalized they were seldom viewed as distinct processes. Awareness, which was defined as knowing through perception or rational process, I considered tangible, thus more accessible. On the other hand, consciousness— knowing through instinct or intuition—I considered intangible. It was a simple distinction, to be sure, but for overcoming inherited limitations and inducing change, it was important. Awareness became the means with which consciousness was expanded. Once exercise, diet, meditation, and lifestyle were unified, awareness so heightened psychophysiological sensibility that greater consciousness could be realized, or employed. *Yet all four aspects had to be unified.* The problem was that few people realized the power that could result from unification; it was too easy to be drawn into extremes. With each action enthusiasm and idealism had to be wisely refined.

Although my faith in Adidas running shoes could never be shaken, I soon learned the best way to exercise was to artfully combine running with a selection of yogic postures and strict attention to breathing. Breathing, the key to fitness, provided a means of managing the inner dimensions of attitude. How and why exercise was performed was as important as how much was completed or with what intensity it was executed. I found it was best to exercise alone, early in the morning, because separate time had to be devoted to stress relaxation, preferably later in the day.

Daily exercise might be occasionally sacrificed to weather or business, but the need to control consumption and attend to stress relaxation should never be ignored. I learned to be wary of the dictatorial tone of nutritionists who seemed more interested in establishing salable reputations than dealing with the complexity of consumption. Popular diet books generated greater sales than those dealing with running, yoga, and meditation combined, but their success was due to the fact that most nutritionists (or their publishers) shrewdly focused on the weight reduction aspect of diet, because, next to credit, fat was the most pernicious problem in America. Kenneth Pelletier highlighted some of the confusion:

> Complex biochemical processes take place constantly in all the cells of our bodies. In order for these to continue, a variety of nutrients must always be present in adequate amounts. Beyond this single point of agreement, the field of nutrition and health fragments into a morass of strident opinions based upon little or no empirical data, and dietary prescriptions which are frequently totally contradictory.

The optimum goal seemed to be some kind of final lifetime diet, one limited to a nourishing assortment of basic foods, which avoided most of the hazards of consumption while increasing awareness of what was consumed. Never rigid, a final lifetime diet always considered the gender, age, occupation, and special stress of the home and work-place, and was to be slowly implemented into individual lifestyle; it recognized the value of growing and preparing one's own food whenever possible, and above all recognized the need to fast regularly.

The trick was to ignore fads.

I found few fixed rules except that any health problems had to be carefully considered, and fasts had to fit individual needs. Planning when and why to fast was wise, and extremes were to be avoided. A day without food or liquids, or a day or two without either was sufficient. The basic objective of fasting was not only to rest the digestive system, but to secure freedom from the tyranny of consumption and the dictatorial web of reward foolish consumption perpetuated. Only after this was recognized could beneficial removal be secured. Removal—freedom from the patterns of habit—was the key to awareness. Removal, the ability to disengage from the demanding network of daily involvement, facilitated *seeing* and inspired actualization, that need to "get into something," even a silent dinner party.

To establish a final lifetime diet, a wise first step was eliminating red meat and red meat products, because the nutritional benefits of meat could be supplied by other foods. Meat was not only a difficult food to digest, but the source of fatal fats, questionable additives, and dangerous carcinogens. Other dietary dangers—salt, white sugar, and excessive dairy products—had to be minimized, along with refined grains. Once these basic adjustments were made, a final lifetime diet became a triumph of conviction and victory over the tyranny of processed foods; it also limited consumption to fresh fruits and vegetables, whole grains, legumes, occasional nuts, dairy, chicken or fish, and herb teas. Despite the varieties, this kind of diet could become somewhat boring. The saving grace was to rely on raw or natural foods as much as possible, and rigorously examine belief in minimum daily requirements and other nutritional folklore that maliciously played upon the connection between mindless consumption and good health, a crime against culture if ever there was one.

Developing a habit of meditation, perhaps the most important quadrant in the action quartet, at least for spiritual renewal, was more complex. Time had to be managed, and the mind needed the will to sort through conflicting information and to overcome the insistence of those who rejected the idea of nondenominational meditation. Developing meditation meant suffering a grueling initiation interrupted by itches and tickles and flashes of laundry, unmade phone calls, the Shah of Iran, the need to buy fresh bread, erotic phantoms, Vietnam body counts, unpaid bills, or more phantoms. The object was to turn off the mind's perpetual motion, to discover how meditation restored tranquility and signaled the ultimate migration back to the self.

> Meditation has been misunderstood in this country, especially because of the simplified commercialized versions. . . . People have come to regard it as sort of 15 minutes of drugless bliss . . . [but] that's not really what meditation is about. Meditation is a way of reorganizing oneself internally, psychologically, emotionally, and even, perhaps, spiritually, if you can use that word without making it religious.

Rudolph Ballentine's definition was apt, certainly more democratic than most, implying that meditation was accessible to anyone who had the patience to pursue it. Religious or organizational aids were quite unnecessary, for the origin of meditation was unknown. Its tradition was as ancient in the West as in the East; like wonder, it was a natural gift obscured by the very glut of din it alone could assuage.

There was only one requirement: that the individual regularly withdraw, seek a quiet place, sit on a chair, the floor, a bed, or a cushion, and simply stop. Close the eyes, still the body, and empty the mind. This was not easy but, once accomplished, produced a state in which the dimensions of removal became real—irrevocably fixed. Just as silent dinners proved how much could be heard without speech, meditation proved how much could be seen with the eyes closed.

If meditation was the most intriguing action in the quartet, lifestyle was the most ambiguous and the one most commonly subjected to tinny interpretations. An independent, individual lifestyle had to be patiently designed, for it was most easily disrupted. So few seemed to realize that only an independent way of life, free of technological distraction, could produce the removal necessary to evaluate the intricately wired web in which modern existence was ensnared. Until the individual had the opportunity to make this evaluation, individual existence was limited to levels of ordinary awareness, and the potential of consciousness remained a remote enigma. There were innumerable ways to evaluate lifestyle. But in serious survey, the self, through which the soul existed, was eventually seen as a fabric of selves, or past lives—a living presence whose gender, roots, race, family background, religious and cultural influence, and education defined that presence at any point in time. Accepting the importance of mystery, this survey revealed the myriad ways lifestyle was woven into circles of attachments and relationships that were shaped by material needs, geography, and the diverse circumstance of chance and change. Individual lifestyle was determined by work and the presence of friends, a lover or a spouse, children— or the desire for children—family, and peer groups. It was shaped by culture, travel, and inquiry, and limited by the character of society and the degree of isolation from nature. Above all, lifestyle was complicated by inordinate exposure to modern persuasion—television, telephone, computer, radio, mail, newspapers, periodicals, and the other unnatural shocks to which the American was a particularly harried heir. Out of this immense mix, individual lifestyle not only had to be defined and maintained, but reclaimed and revised in order that deeper recognitions could occur, recognitions that could easily diminish patriotism or alter the qualities of passion.

The secret was never to stand in line for anything.

It was important to loathe credit, but more important to develop free will, without which a unique lifestyle was impossible. The perennial problem was to see beyond immediate existence and develop the confidence to discard useless attachments and sever negative relationships. Sorting out questionable clutter was imperative; every American life seemed burdened with too many objects and too many people. Yet selectivity could be agonizing. It could seem almost as difficult to discard a favorite coat or an unused electric carving knife as it was to file for divorce or drop peevish relatives—those who would not sympathize with the demands of change or who would perversely choose to subvert it. There were no fixed formulas, or guaranteed methods; separate realities came out of actions that altered ordinary awareness and justified the complex utilization of loneliness.

The demands of a revised lifestyle were often painful and riddled with a weird futility that invaded the common hour. I remember one particularly lovely afternoon when I parked my brown Mercury and noticed that the speedometer had reached 85,007 miles. As I stared at the numbers, the indented display became a fixed oval illuminated by light from the sunroof. Later that night I figured that in 7 years, if I averaged 20 miles per hour in combined city and freeway driving, I had spent 4250 hours, or 177 days, or 25 weeks—a full 6 months of my life sitting in the driver's seat of that vehicle. I feared even worse numbers for the amount of time I had spent in front of the television. In either case it was more time than I had spent exercising, fasting, meditating, or avoiding rash people and all of the other modern persuasions that flooded my lifestyle.

To expect the truth to come from thinking signifies that we mistake the need to think with the urge to know.

—Hannah Arendt

The final effect of my visit to Mad Bear was that it reduced the immediacy of publishing and revived my need to act *into* something. I decided to make a retreat, but was deliberate about selecting a time and place. Because of my ongoing web of commitments, a retreat was not easy to arrange, but it seemed to be the only way to purposely seek out *otherness*, or the only way in which levels of ordinary awareness might be isolated and examined.

I chose a full-mooned week and, fasting from food, talk, the telephone, television, radio, and even books, I saw no one for five days. Toward the end of the second evening I broke down and drank two glasses of juice, and on the fourth morning I ate a half of pink grapefruit. After surviving the initial loneliness and the stomach's crude rebellion when its rewards were interrupted, I settled into a light peace of mind. Unfortunately, the atmosphere did not disguise the limitations of the action quartet. I began to see that in some ways the unification of awareness that I was attempting only provided a diversion (albeit beneficial) from the confusion of consciousness. Converting issues of conduct, health, faith, and ecology into individual actions offered a certain alternative from the domination of traditional authority, but as the hours of retreat slipped into evenings and mornings, it was impossible to ignore the fact that the root confusion—the mystery of consciousness—still haunted every effort. If psychologists, physicians, clergy, and scientists could not resolve schisms or deal with holistic well-being, could I, after pink grapefruit, resolve the crisis?

The last evening, during a bright moon vigil, I fell into a deep sleep and woke before dawn; a nearby field seemed inhabited even though no one was there. At first the ambivalence was so refreshing it seemed comic—then melancholy—then immaterial. Sitting in the quiet grass, I spent the morning contemplating free will and the power of choosing. But choosing what? So indulgently isolated, so close to the narcissistic edge, I chose not to choose, a particular luxury that did little to deal with mystery or reduce spiritual uncertainty. Consequently the hours went by as shade slid across the secluded field. I tried to study the composition of my feelings and examine the quality or structure of otherness, only to find that otherness had no structure.

It was not until I reviewed the brain/mind question that I was able to fix attention. Because it was believed the brain stored the memories of a lifetime, I wondered if it did not store the memories of other lives as well. It occurred to me to connect the present with an unlimited past, with the collective unconscious. In previous months I had begun to study reincarnation but, like quantum physics or brain radiation, the subject was vast and complex. Hindu thought unconditionally accepted reincarnation, as did Buddhism—early Buddhism, Mahayana and Tibetan Buddhism. The early Egyptians, Romans, and Greeks accepted it; so did some cabalistic, Christian, and Islamic literature; so did the Masons and Theosophists. In studying reincarnation the contradiction of religious doctrines was disconcerting but, removed by the retreat, the distinction between the intellectual consideration and a more live realization of my own past became apparent. I began to visualize a gap between consideration and realization and, as I did, the distinction slowly dissolved and allowed a new sense of self to emerge. I began to imagine the repetition of births, lives, and deaths—the continual development the soul must experience in order to be liberated from the blind level on which ordinary life seemed so freakishly confined. By evening, in the chilled stillness and contours of imagination and feeling, I recognized the possibility that *the life I was living I had lived before and would live again and again.* This verified the realization that all of my hate, all of my love and greed and hope had been experienced before and would be experienced again, which in turn provided graceful relief from trial and trouble. But exactly how to employ that relief—in such a way that the past equaled the present and helped resolve the future—was unresolved.

The following day I returned home, resumed work, and had to adjust to the responsibilities of ordinary awareness. One associate had returned from a trek in Nepal and another from traffic court in Oakland. I could not expect anyone to understand where I had been, but I tried to gradually tell them about the retreat and the effects of my recognition of my own past lives. This was a mistake. After a few moments of polite and sober attention, the discussion became almost giddy. Someone mentioned how ironic it was that reincarnation pervaded early Christian life, yet was so absent from modern tradition, but this was flushed away by talk of "the karma that connects souls and creates affinity between lovers." Once this was mentioned, the conversation exploded with all kinds of embarrassing New Age claims—silly suppositions that previous lives had been spent as butterflies, seagulls, leopards, or a host of Renaissance aristocrats or praetorian guards. I said nothing more but recalled how Jack Schwarz, spiritual adept and founder of the Aletheia Foundation, often mused about the number of people who claimed relationship with Egyptian royalty in previous incarnations. In years of consultations he had dealt with countless memories of queens and pharaohs, but had never met anyone who had labored on the pyramids.

As time passed and my study continued, I became more objective and speculative. Belief that upon entering each life the soul was afforded the opportunity to pick parents in order to work out past karma seemed reasonable, and infant crib death, thought by some to be the newborn's rejection of the choice of life, became plausible. The difficulty was that such theories were classified as occult folklore, phenomena that did not merit serious scientific attention. Nevertheless, such speculation disclosed the difference between understanding a theory and implementing its use. Once this was recognized, understanding could be dramatically increased. If the life I was leading had been led before, then I had faced every trial and tribulation. As the ramifications of this idea became clear, all of the urgencies of my everyday existence were reduced and all of the intimidation and confusion seemed more manageable. Considering this, I could not help but wonder whether this was the reason that reincarnation as a reality was as intriguing as it was; it relieved real as well as imagined problems. Even death itself, "the great distinguished thing," as Henry James had called it, had been experienced over and over again. Because of this recognition every soft or shocking end, every pain and passion, became less significant. The insanity of nuclear threat, the bitter bends of business, the fear of aging, loneliness, cancer, crime, even the delicate needs of an adolescent daughter began to fade. My life and the lives of those I knew became historical scenes of the soul—revues that opened with birth, closed with death, and opened again to revive, at long last, the grandeur of spirituality and the union of the soul with the common hour.

Yet the immediacy of past lives was not always inspiring; often it seemed a fictitious condition made real only by the rewards of seeing and understanding. Despite the change in my awareness, I had reached no Olympian height and still had not broken some inner, insidious mesh of stress that seemed to permeate every feeling. It was mindless to complain that America was a stressful place in which to live, a culture of chance in which finer sensibilities were ultimately subverted. The curse was the blessing. In America, change and chance provided dazzling opportunity and reward, and though no one denied the stress it produced, few knew what to do about it. In *Mind As Healer, Mind As Slayer*, a holistic approach to the prevention of stress disorder—the title was derived from a Zen saying—Kenneth Pelletier warned how stress could build from youth into a "slow, developmental accumulation . . . throughout life." There were no simple solutions. To be sure, exercise and a control of consumption produced profound relief, yet neither could completely satisfy that inner core. Documenting the relationship between stress and distress, Pelletier reviewed the basic methods of controlling it: biofeedback, autogenic training, and meditation; of the three the latter was most appealing. Meditation required no technology and minimal outside support. The meditator was not only able to do something *for* the self before doing anything *with* the self, but had a unique, individual link with mystery, the source of spiritual renewal. That link seemed anchored in the mind . . . in some limitless ocean that was as fearful or grand as imagination allowed . . . some edge where neurotic subversion and foul climates of loneliness, doubt, and fear could be traced back to the kiva of the soul . . . where, colored and scarred by previous lives, the splayed connections eventually wove into every living heartbeat and brain wave. Only through meditation did it seem possible to inventory this history and all of its traded impressions and begin to right ancient wrong.

Eventually I began to take greater advantage of meditation, even while continuing to suffer the irritation of business and the dreadful risk of that "slow, developmental accumulation" that might eventually strike me down with a gruesome heart attack. (In an oblique way, however, a heart attack was preferable to seeing the hope of a naturally orchestrated death ruined by ubiquitous cancer or some other bit of punk luck.) At any rate, it soon became unthinkable to let a day pass without "separating" myself for thirty or forty minutes. During these separations I was free to retreat and recall every job, every school I had attended, every Christmas . . . free to conduct imaginary tours through all of the rooms, apartments, and houses I had ever inhabited . . . city by neighborhood, street by door, year by day, until I was able to disappear into familiar woodlands or ride another huge green streetcar past the shadows of screened porches and the sloping lawns of Hanscome Park in the Omaha of my childhood.

Because the benefits of meditation were cumulative, increased effort could break through previous limits and allow for experiment and experience. Propped comfortably on a pillow in a stilled room and staring into a mirror hung some eighteen or twenty inches from the face could produce striking results. After fifteen or twenty minutes, my reflected image came alive and the room faded. After a longer while the expression of the reflection alternated between flashes of sadness and innocence or changed into grotesque forms that varied in their expressions between hostility and love . . . each rebelling against the other. If I resisted one likeness, it might disintegrate or swell until my eyes bled away or my nose narrowed and my face billowed with the rise and fall of every breath. In my journal I tried to document this, but the entries never conveyed the experience satisfactorily. In a strange way I seemed inhibited by the fact that in America meditation was considered strictly a religious exercise, not a device of illumination or psychic recognition. Few seemed to profit from the double bounty, and few were inclined to correct the misunderstanding or campaign for the reconstruction of the wasted or misused morning. It was ironic that those most familiar with meditation were outside of the network of popular communication and remained outside expressly to distance themselves from contemporary confusion.

Meditation was a necessary device, especially when it came time to evaluate the need for a spiritual teacher or guide. It was difficult for me to accept the idea of a single source of authority, almost impossible to see how spiritual renewal could come from Western-style evangelism or Eastern arrivals, some of whom, it was discovered, were not only guilty of economic coercion but of making sexual demands on attractive female followers. Yet such disenchantment did not diminish my respect for the teacher or the guide. Either could be invaluable, although it was wise for the concerned individual to first explore the idea of spiritual renewal before making any commitment. Time after time my own investigation confirmed the suspicion that if a teacher or a guide was needed—or inexplicably appeared—there would be little hesitation or lack of recognition.

Living teachers were not difficult to come by, though the disciplined structure of the teaching process sometimes conflicted with the psychophysiological change brought on by increased awareness and consciousness. Guides, figures, or voices from within, were more prized. They furnished a more romantic authority and reduced the tyranny of traditional influence. Yet, in light of modern problems, the concerned individual had to be wary. It was the worst of times to trust, but the best of times to open the self to wonder and the faith that the desire for change would eventually produce change. But before wonder or faith, the role of the teacher or real or imagined guide had to be understood; more, a fundamental familiarity with power, purification, and protection had to be fully appreciated.

All guides possessed power but not every guide was willing to lead or able to inspire. Some were bankrupt on levels beyond one's immediate understanding; others were simply unwilling to carry out the delicate task of revealing ways through the maze of confusion that fogged ordinary awareness. The guide's gift was an obscure gift, one that required a sure control of energy and amazing grace. Outside the organized influence of religion—with which the solitary guide was seldom concerned—the role offered few, if any, dividends. The power of the solitary guide was always poorly defined and often perversely fictionalized, but its effects could be useful to those who were properly fascinated. The problem was that fascination was a faint prelude to revelation that could never be scheduled or guaranteed. All that could be expected of inquiry into this power was the confirmation of mystery, after which the concerned individual was free to risk levels of larger life. To accomplish this it was necessary to successfully *go within*. In the beginning I avoided other students and dedicated followers and rigorously resisted any pressure. Every suspicion had to be respected; whenever there were recurring doubts, the wise move was to go beyond shadows of authority.

The difficulty was that for many people the fascination with power became a burdensome and sometimes fatal temptation. Although it should have been obvious that power could rarely be duplicated or secured through parochial means, it was disappointing how many tried to appropriate it. There were always unfortunates who tried to go beyond safe limits of understanding and assumed roles for which they were not at all prepared, not at all qualified. The fabrications that resulted from such deviation were usually mundane or embarrassing, but occasionally—if too far from the foundation of truth and love—set off action and reaction that created cruel disappointment or turmoil. In New Age theaters there were minor concessions that traded on various projections of power. It was an inept exchange, but often the consequences, however fatuously or famously employed, became contaminated or fatally flawed. Homemade efforts at exertion or exorcism usually produced weird reactions that eventually ruptured experimenters. After a while, they might begin to suffer from unexpected exposure to negative elements or a peculiar disorientation that drained energy and left them stale, sad figures.

True guides, unmistakable talents, avoided theaters. Though capable of creating stages if they were needed, they usually chose rare or remote arenas in which to cross power with *time, place,* and *need* to obtain an artful *balance* between the positive and negative results of each. This was active use of the ancient sanctity of fourness—the four elements, four seasons, or four directions—fundamental interchange that could reveal ways and means of psychic purification or protection. I never found a dependable guide nor was I inspired to seek a teacher; perhaps this was a mistake or perhaps my own involvement offered enough wonder. I could never be certain. Through meditation and controlled removal, I did discover inner guides or guiding forces whose influence could never be anticipated, yet I tried not to delude myself about these. Guiding forces could often be mistaken for fantasies. Periodically I suspected they were particles of past or future spirits or extensions of those selves I had observed in mirrored meditation. Seldom isolated or confirmed, they usually remained fluid imprints that reinforced my awareness of the need for sober speculation.

At this point recognition of psychic purification and the particulars of protection became important. Nonobjective *use* of purification and protection benefited the development of awareness, and a nonobjective *sense* of both was indispensable to greater consciousness. I found it was best to keep them separate and consider purification first. Purification lightened and clarified climates of inquiry and helped eliminate irritating obstruction and obscurity. More of a female activity, it refined that indefinable use of energy upon which higher understanding seemed to depend. Protection, a tougher, more male matter, had to be strictly controlled and continually reviewed and modified. Protection was best implemented through device or visualization and this required a certain humility and certainly an expensive use of time and effort.

There were various ways to employ purification. Candles, incense, houseplants, and talismans of all kinds could be employed; the power of purification, however, came more from the *intention* than the use. The visualization of a blue or gold fog or soft imaginary rain not only cleansed and clarified psychic perception and physical atmospheres but also improved attitude.

Taking measures of protection helped ensure against negative or disrupting influence outside the range of normal perception. Protection was best viewed as a *design* rather than a defense against disruptive forces or rude interference. Because negative interference was often attracted to positive activity, the need for psychic protection was as great as the need for psychological independence or physical insurance against the invasion of dangerous persuasion. Like purification, protection could be invoked by tangibles or a talisman or by a simple visualization, the effects of which were better experienced than described. But protection demanded more complex concentration and required greater sensitivity to the complications of attachments and relationships from which difficulty usually arose. Whether negation grew out of present associations or past involvement, it was best to limit protection to tangible levels, where it could interact with interference; it was useless to try to protect hopes or ideas. Like purification, the effects of protection could be endlessly compounded by serious intention.

I confirmed the benefits of purification and protection when I began to experiment with a yogic position known as shavasana, or corpse pose. Lying flat on my back in a secluded, quiet area, I spread my arms and legs and, with the palms of my hands facing upward and my eyes closed, carefully and slowly regulated the rhythm of breathing—*always from* the abdomen and *only through* the nose—until, lying perfectly still, I could maintain the position for at least thirty to forty minutes. (It was important to use a coverlet of some kind, because as the circulatory and respiratory systems slowed, the temperature of the body fell, and it was easy to suffer a chill.) After a while this became easy, but extending the time beyond forty minutes proved difficult, and it took months of practice before I was able to lie still for more than fifty or sixty minutes. The trick was not to move or fall asleep, although if I became quite sleepy, it was best to accept it rather than deny the fatigue. The benefits were incalculable.

Once perfected and practiced regularly, meditative relaxation in this asana not only magnified visualization but was an incredible means of relieving stress and energizing the body. After fifteen or twenty minutes of stillness, tension seemed to filter off the arms, legs, and chest, but the degree of relaxation could be deceptive. Occasionally, after thirty or forty minutes, a wrist or ankle might suddenly twitch—recoiling from a release of buried tension. Nonetheless, when a truly deep meditative state was attained, anxiety was further diffused and feelings and thoughts could be patiently dismissed or reviewed. Alien interference of negative people could be recognized and, once located, isolated in a precise manner; purifying and protective visualizations could then be utilized to disperse it. Carefully colored counterclockwise circles could be slowly drawn around the interference and the gyrations accelerated until it could be spun off and sent back to its source. After a timeless pause a purifying fog could be washed into the void, where—visualizing each half-breath as a single brush stroke—a wide, five-pointed star could be drawn across affected areas and then allowed to hang before dissolving into the body or space.

Circles and stars were simple symbols of protection that could be used in countless ways. A star drawn across a window or door could ensure against physical or psychic intrusion. But of course any such visualization hardly substituted for a simple lock or the wisdom of avoiding or retreating from shadowed or dangerous areas.

Clockwise visualization was positive. The *clockwise circle* could be used to focus on a situation or a particular person who needed to be scrutinized; sympathetically colored it would become a means of sending love or trust to someone in need. Reversed, the circle became defensive; drawn *counterclockwise* in hard colors it could neutralize suspected influence, obstruct rage or jealousy, or offset insidious intrusion that resulted from exchange with rash people or unexpected turmoil. Despite the advantages it was wise to remember these measures were only symbolic and their effectiveness always depended on clear, honest intention. What was difficult to understand was the extent to which protection demanded sympathy and love. It could never be successfully used to condemn or secure advantage of any kind, especially material. To be effective the intent of protection, like that of purification, had to originate in truth and had to be removed from desire. Misused, it could be the source of dangerous reaction which, once inspired, could quickly subvert understanding.

While exploring these reaches I discovered more startling uses of the corpse pose, but such discovery required restraint, for they were susceptible to the same burdensome temptation that surrounded power. After a period of planned removal (a day or two of silence and fasting), it was possible to maintain the pose for seventy or eighty minutes. By then the systems of the body had become so relaxed that the feeling of the floor faded, and the effect of breathing was negligible; even the slowed beating of the heart seemed to melt away. In this extreme, if the stillness was successfully maintained, it was possible to experiment with separating the self from the body. On rare occasions my body began to sink as if it were being lowered from some intangible association with the self. This kind of division needed to be delicately focused, for repossession of the body could prove difficult. To extend the separation or try to meditate *during* the separation was a maneuver that could be frightening and difficult to correct. It was wise to avoid such gymnastics and simply be content with sorting fears or studying the dimensions of the altered state—assessment of the difference between ordinary awareness and those levels on which illumination became a connection with transcendence . . . became a phantasm from which it seemed possible to peer into endless centers of nothing-ness—views limited by fear but views so wondrous that they put into perspective the gross ocean of psychic con-fusion and the pathetic material insistence in which ordi-nary awareness was imprisoned and which only spiritual renewal could repair.

*Because of impatience we were driven from Eden
and because of impatience we cannot return.*
                                    —*Franz Kafka*

Crow was of the opinion that spiritual renewal, "if there is such a thing," required more than psychophysiological well-being and "the heady acrobatics of nondenominational meditation. You've a tendency to forget that determining psychological or physical condition is always a presumption and that meditation is an enigmatic device."

I feared he was right, but to discuss the matter further I had to write letters. A year or so after I remarried he began wandering again, and the immediacy of our companionship dissolved as it had when I had left New York in the mid-1950s. Whenever I needed advice or wanted a reaction, I wrote to an address in Los Angeles, somewhere below Griffith Park, or left a telephone message at one of two general stores up the California coast, one near Mendocino and one near Little River. He always answered. If the need was urgent he seemed to know. Once, when I was snarled in a galling contract dispute, he sensed my predicament and called collect at 6:00 A.M. from Parowan, Utah, of all places. Before I even had a chance to explain the matter, he suggested the solution, and then launched into an impressive monologue about the need for letting go and transcending petty involvement, warning that in the 1990s it would be imperative to remain detached from the material. "The secret is selectivity! Pick out important problems— then ask the right questions. Don't fight the wrong war."

In order to apply this advice to spiritual renewal, I tried to separate the actualization of transcendence from dogma and begin to see it as an integral part of removal. I was not being frivolous; actualization of transcendence was a kind of consolidation of change, but how religious could I be? There seemed no point between dogma and mystery where a nondenominational approach was seriously considered, and even in New Age circles there were few to which to turn. I had little rapport with revised Christians and found it impossible to relate to either traditional or disenchanted Catholics, most of whom seemed to suffer from some odd fear that outside the Church, change would lead to quicker cancer. When I sought to define transcendence in nondenominational terms, I found those concerned with Eastern alternatives equally myopic. Enmeshed in vedas, miracles, or Buddhism, most were too burdened to bother with comparative perspective.

What I was seeking was some way to actualize transcendence, but when I tried to do this I often felt as if I were starting over. Somehow when I was a boy in Omaha, transcendence was never difficult. It was easily achieved through simply climbing a tree or through launching imagination by whirling whole new worlds out of the spin of dizzy games! As I grew older I lost this power and began to doubt. . . . I seldom knew what or why. As an altar boy I overindulged in the drama of the Mass, wore the serious starched white surplice over black or red cassocks, and, with other towheads, got stoically stoned during Benediction . . . swinging swirling fumes from the silver incense burner toward old Irish women who sat in tearful lines of discomfort in front pews, pinching their faces more than their rosaries. There was little appreciation of *seeing* then, and no way to realize the enormous change that would have to occur before I could discover that altered states did not necessarily ensure transcendence.

It was a mistake made by most.

Only by laboring through the agony of change and the illusory elaboration of refined meditation did I see that to renew spirituality it was necessary to transcend ordinary awareness with great deliberation; only then could the instant or decade be evaluated in the light of infinite wonder. The problem was that the potential of transcendence was as rigidly regulated by religious dogma as material belief systems were reinforced by scientific determinism. Dogma and determinism restricted spiritual experience and limited awareness and—for the serious seeker—limited the understanding of altered states by creating dread of any departure from ordinary awareness. Loss of ordinary awareness threatened the security of inherited patterns of recognition. By going outside these patterns, a seeker jeopardized the reality in which ordinary awareness was founded. Condemned by many as a living sleep or the paralysis of forgetfulness, ordinary awareness still constituted fundamental everyday reality, and the possibility of losing it accentuated fears that it could be sensibly recovered. Yet, despite fears, distortions, and social prohibitions, the desire to alter awareness was an instinctual demand that haunted every human being. Transcendence was a universal temptation, a primordial need; it was the existential link with mystery that no prohibition could deter. The pragmatic solution was to seek transcendence through organized religious devotion, but this required questionable identification and submission to authority. And outside organized religion, transcendence required degrees of cultural isolation and intense dedication few were capable of producing. Nevertheless, because of my conviction that the life I was leading I had led before, I was convinced that, out of the need for spiritual renewal that change produced, ordinary awareness could be judiciously altered and frontiers of consciousness patiently explored.

The fear of altered states always seemed ironic to me, because our ordinary awareness was continually altered by a variety of natural highs—often without any recognition of what occurred and usually without any consideration of transcendence. Ordinary awareness could be altered by the roar of a crowd or a flush of solitary intention, the combustion of competition or the satisfying release of rewarding work. Awareness could be altered by the magic of music or the energy of love and sex—or love—or sex—any sorcery of flesh. Alterations, or highs, were produced by hate, power, or the acquisition of money, but were most widely produced through common consumption. It took years for the public to recognize the extent to which refined white sugar rushed the blood, produced false, expensive energy, and, ever so slightly, altered awareness. It took almost as long to recognize the narcosis produced by caffeine and nicotine. These were minor alterations, changes that society had decided were legally acceptable.

Awareness was altered by alcohol, marijuana, and many tolerated devices that, for better or worse, relieved the demand of instinctual needs. Legal or not, drugs were the primary means of alteration of consciousness, vehicles capable of dissolving daily concern and gradually evaporating time and space. Yet drugs were unreliable and manipulation of usage never truly effective; procedures that worked once eventually failed faithful repetition. Alcohol was the most popular device, but its misuse was holocaustal. More than a million Americans were killed or maimed annually in automobile accidents involving alcohol, and half of all drowning and fire victims were intoxicated when they awoke (or never awoke) in water or flames. This tragic tally was only part of an unofficial horde that, according to Lester Grinspoon of Harvard, "could be just as well called alcohol addicts." Oddly enough, because of the power of the liquor lobby in Congress, alcohol was never officially listed as a drug under the Food, Drug, and Cosmetic Act. Other legal alterations were afforded by tranquilizers and stimulants, but many doubted the benefits. In the late 1970s FDA Commissioner Jere E. Goyen warned that nearly five billion legal tranquilizers were being consumed annually. The magnitude of such abuse obscured the instinctual demand for transcendence and tended to ascribe to states of ordinary awareness a substantiality they might not otherwise have. But on the frontiers of consciousness, where the transcendence of ordinary awareness was addressed, the problems were equally obscure.

Individual and collective attempts at transcendence, however well-intended or passionate, often lacked a necessary cohesiveness or disintegrated into unfortunate conflict. Beyond levels of ordinary awareness, where exploration of altered states became more native or savage (depending on the sympathy of the observer) there was other disgraceful abuse and misuse of drugs. On these illegal levels the quality of device was always unpredictable and the terrain of involvement deceptive. The only certainty was that being so removed from the quality control that legal drugs had, the potential of the high could not be calculated and experiment could turn riotous. At any unexpected or promising rise, the experimenter's control could suddenly disintegrate into dangerous depths or soar away over heights without warning—instantly disrupting balance and sensations of color or temperature. Then the hope for transcendence was sacrificed for sanity and survival in melted horizons, frontiers from which there was no guarantee of safe return. Little could be done for these "pioneers" and even less for burnouts. Transcendence could be ruptured by obnoxious speed freaks, LSD ghouls, ketamine users, or inhibited by those who tried to "squirm out of the self" through cocaine—the crystal snow, the soundless jazz valued at seven times the price of gold and blatantly used by artists, musicians, lawyers, doctors, and an assorted coterie who could not resist its succulent mesmerization. Instead of providing transcendence, cocaine magnified material confidence and ignited sexuality until judgment was eroded and bloated reaction overran reality. By then the attraction of transcendence was reduced to folly. But where did the folly begin? I wondered if it was not rooted in that childhood need for the magic of dizzy games or programmed into the brain by thousands of sugared pauses that refreshed. I wondered if it was not, as most dedicated observers claimed, simply a misguided backlash against authority. Whatever the reasons, in some respect the folly reflected a New Age failure.

It seemed as meaningless to protest the hypocritical use of scientifically approved drugs as it was to lament the tragedy of illegal wastelands, for it was the responsibility of the serious seeker to avoid ironies and search for the tracks of more sophisticated travelers who had passed frontiers and wastelands and reached more austere levels, where intention was free of illusion. There device was never used to combat confusion. To reach such levels the traveler had to have learned how greater consciousness was realized through the freedom of exceeding the single self and seeking that sacred silence that was always most threatened from the left. Yet how many could carry inquiry so far without guidance or religious support?

Crow wrote that the intelligent use of drugs was "the most existential and economic way to alter awareness and begin spiritual renewal, if that's needed." He did not dismiss religious or nondenominational renewal, but insisted that "most of those who truly try will come—after many odd progressions—to the need for mescaline or some other 'divine food' in order to achieve any transcendence." When I questioned his belief that drugs were necessary, he insisted that in order to alter awareness and begin meaningful transcendence, there had to be some crucible. He agreed a radical renovation of lifestyle was vital, but insisted that the pious use of a powerful device could also be essential. Extolling psilocybin, he wrote that

> with synthesized psilocybin, it's easier to take advantage of recognition of the altered state and avoid the rutting retch which sometimes comes from eating peyote buttons, stone-ground paste or various concoctions . . . even though these discomforts are incidental if the wonder of traditional ceremony can be enjoyed—but that's a rare event.

In a subsequent letter, when he reiterated the need for "the splendor of induced hallucination!" I replied that a patient practice of meditation might be preferable to such splendor, but he feared that

before you're able to turn modern lifestyle around toward spiritual renewal, media and materialism might well do you in. In order to avoid this, it's necessary to successfully *pass through* the trial of hallucination.

To do this you need to remember three things. The first is to be prepared for the ugly mush of puritanistic guilt and fear which will flood up from the subconscious and be mistaken for hallucination. The second is to realize that experience and reaction to the experience are *different* recognitions. And the third is to see that conditions—no matter how psychedelic—are incomparable and, on high levels, a result of reaction of the living self to previous selves and other worlds.

In order to manage this experience and go beyond reaction, you must sort through these contradictions. But the ways and means of doing so cannot be fixed, for once the high begins it becomes necessary to adjust to whatever conditions it produces. This is where romanticists get into trouble. Since these adjustments can be devilishly delightful, they find it more fun to just ingest and trip out! Trying in a single sunrise or sunset to make a Shangrila out of a Sausalito or a Taos is a feat I've never seen accomplished. The important thing is to be able to use a device to induce hallucination while, *at the same time*, shedding that use in order to react . . . without being washed into the splatter of distortion that can awe and terrorize *at the same time*. This requires a physical disassociation and an inner, psychic comprehension of sensation and impression. To accurately assess hallucinatory variations and reap

the reward of controlling the high in order to see beyond it, it's necessary to trust in the purity of the device as well as its source and—more importantly—
have faith in the intention of such a journey. This is
sophisticated travel, but not impossible.

I was convinced he spoke from experience, but there
were flaws—ones that could be found in most of the early
drug literature. The writings of DeQuincey and Baude-
laire, though sensational when they first appeared, seemed
tame in the 1980s when it became apparent that with both
writers the effects were more important than the reason for
consumption. Even the considerations of William James
and Freud, though more scientifically founded, became
thin contributions once more had been learned about effects. Before and after his experience with cocaine, Freud
was never aware of the role volition could play in securing
an altered state, and along with James he was ignorant of
the fact that the effects of the cocaine high could be measured only subjectively *at the time* by the user.

In *The Natural Mind* Andrew Weil warned that drugs
could keep people from reaching "the goal of consciousness developed to its highest potential." Weil agreed drugs
altered states of ordinary awareness, but said that at the
same time they tended to support the illusion that the
change came from an external, not internal reality. He
found it "ironic that persons who have the most positive
experience with drugs may also become the ones most enmeshed in illusionary ways of thinking about their own
minds." But even Weil seemed to overlook the fact that the
use of any device, even meditation, was subjective and had
unknown, chameleon qualities. Results and rewards varied

and were always uncertain. Only after altering awareness, crossing frontiers, and mastering hallucination could the successful seeker hope to meet that experienced traveler for whom time and place became a kind of elliptical transition that antiquated illusion and disclosed a familiar cosmos.

PART THREE

FULL CIRCLE

[Prince Amerigo's] future might be scientific. There was nothing in himself, at all events, to prevent it. He was allying himself to science, for what was science but the absence of prejudice backed by the presence of money.

—Henry James

After all was said, after all my observations and experiments, I began to see change differently. I realized I would never be able to practice all that I might preach or accurately preach all that I might practice. The most serious obstacles to the understanding of consciousness were still materialism, the tyranny of social authority, and the fact that many forces were beyond human control. Otherness and the inviting edge of mystery were as remote as the enigma of death.

I had traded in my brown Mercury. The day I did, I remembered that, thirty years before, when I had returned from the Korean War, the idea of an alternative way of life—if considered at all—had largely been treated with ridicule in the United States. Back in New York City I had bought a used Ford convertible and often driven down the West Side Highway from Columbia University to Greenwich Village. Along the Hudson River speckled shards of the Manhattan skyline had risen on my left, and past 79th Street the stacks and decks of the *Queen Mary* had loomed over the elevated roadway like a magnified reflection of elegant promise. A decade before, when my family had moved from Omaha to New York—a transcendence of sorts—ocean liners had been indescribable fascinations that personified the scientific progress of the twentieth century. Forty years later most of them had evaporated into nostalgia, and the docks were in sad repair. More shocking was the extent to which the West Side Highway had rotted away. On December 10, 1973, it had to be closed after a highway department truck plunged through a hole near Gansevoort Street. By 1983 that plunge would have become an omen. The curious thing was that critics took so long to see how such deterioration reflected on science. Science was beyond reproach then.

By the end of the Korean War, scientific authority had prevailed and had prospered; its practitioners had become a cult whose ranks were immune from criticism. If nothing else, immunity was ensured by the utter complexity of scientific initiation and language and the subservience of the media. Idyllic comparisons were endless. Scientists were made out to be a rarefied brotherhood, savants who dealt in miracles, a sacrosanct body to which every element of society deferred. It was an image science did little to discourage. As the decades passed, however, serious doubts began to surface and the image was more shrewdly scrutinized. There were two primary complaints. The first was the refusal of science to own up to the questionable value of many of its miracles, and the second was the failure of scientists to admit that they had little, if any, control over the ultimate consequences of their creations.

Rather than face charges and answer complaints, scientists became more audacious and claimed that any mystery

could be revealed and every problem solved, so long as perennial funding was provided for research. This presumption had been highlighted by an impressive flood of technological wonder before and after World War II. Yet as the
twentieth century passed the midway point and global environmental and economic troubles increased, it became
apparent that much scientific research resulted in needless
development. This conclusion was treated as blasphemy by
scientific apologists, who reacted with disdain to such sug-
gestions and berated critics for a lack of futuristic understanding. For a while apologists could afford to be confident; there was little need to be impartial. Besides, to be
impartial or accept criticism, apologists had to deal with
the supposition that the Age of Science had begun to wane,
and that the future was both not as boundless as had been
supposed and more uncertain. Because of its hauteur,
modern science began to take on an overbearing urgency,
a bloated absolutism. This extravagance inspired more
criticism and a more acute assessment of technology. Faced
with increased ecological awareness, apologists were
forced to deal with a new kind of social disenchantment.
By 1986 confidence in a boundless technological future had
been devastated by a decade of debacle:

- Massive oil rigs had been blown over by ocean winds
  they had been designed "to comfortably withstand."
- Interferon, a highly advertised cure for cancer, had
  proved disappointing. Remissions obtained by the
  "magic bullet" did not seem to last.
- The need had arisen to recall more than a million de-
  fective pacemakers that had been implanted in heart
  patients all over the country.

- Toxic shock death had occurred from synthetic tampons.
- A Union Carbide plant in Bhopal, India, had exploded, killing and maiming more than two thousand people.
- The heralded space shuttle *Challenger* had exploded after lift-off, killing all six crew members and a schoolteacher, the first citizen shot into space.
- In Chernobyl, U.S.S.R., an accident at a nuclear power plant had blown contaminating winds across Europe.

The last event accentuated doubts and gave credence to the growing concern over the development of nuclear weapons, the impact of acid rain, and the outlandish inability of science to deal with nuclear waste. If nuclear war was the hovering menace of the century, acid rain and nuclear waste were ravages that had already arrived. Examining the dreadful spread of radioactive intimidations, Fred Shapiro detailed the horror:

- 2.955 billion cubic feet of uranium mill tailings at forty-four sites;
- 28,315 spent-fuel assemblies; and
- 10.2 million cubic feet of radioactive matter from research and development that increased at the rate of 85,000 cubic feet a year.

And what was to be done with such lethal muck? Official remedies were more surreal than the problem. Some scientists wanted to shoot the stuff into space or dump it in ocean graves near the South Pole. Others thought permanent tombs in Texas the best solution, although the permanency of such tombs could not be guaranteed. Such remedies showed not only the failure of science but also science's arrogant assumption that whatever it did could be undone, or merely tallied as part of the overhead humanity paid for progress. It was a pale specter and caused the concerned individual to begin to question and wonder . . . while passing a schoolyard filled with laughing children or listening in the early morning to the music of birds . . . whether scientific progress was not only a threat to humanity but an insult to human dignity as well.

Behind a last redoubt, scientists often denied direct responsibility for technology, insisting that their only obligation was to the objectivity of dispassionate observation, an almost otherworldly detachment that was allowed to exceed human responsibility because of science's mission to unlock secrets of the universe. But many had pointed out that human progress had not always been the result of science. In 1961 Loren Eiseley noted that several great civilizations had come and gone "without the benefit of a scientific philosophy." Writing about Francis Bacon and postulating that scientific dynamism contained its own doom, Eiseley wrote that science was

> an *invented* cultural institution not present in all societies and not one to be counted upon to arise from human instinct. [It was] as capable of decay and death as any other human activity, such as religion or a system of government. It cannot be equated with individual thought or the unique observations of genius, even though it partakes of these things.

As a way of life, Eiseley wrote, science had to be acquired, its practice "transmitted from generation to generation by the formal process of education." Science, he said, existed "only within a tradition of constant experimental investigation of the natural world," demanding that hypothesis "be subject to proof, whether in nature or in the laboratory," boundaries scientists themselves found extremely difficult to sustain. Science was

> not natural to man at all. It has to be learned, consciously practiced, stripped out of the sea of emotions, prejudices, and wishes in which our daily lives are steeped. No man can long endure such rarified heights without descending to common earth. Even the professional scientist frequently confines such activity to a specific discipline, and outside of it indulges in his illogical prejudices.

Yet most scientists seemed immune to the fear that their discoveries had made the world ugly or dangerous. Apologists still separated science and technology, blaming ecological troubles on the *use* to which technology was applied, and contending that within the confines of pure science dispassionate experiment was inviolate and no one had the right to restrict it.

This was challenged by critics who charged that science had used up its pure confines, that too much contemporary scientific exploration could be traced to exaggerated military needs and self-serving corporate domination of government-financed university research. It had been revealed that in universities the search for holistic cures or a means of prevention of cancer were poorly funded because of the bias of pharmaceutical interests that profited from the emphasis given chemotherapy and radiation—and medicine was only one area affected. Investigating the "laboratory invasion of commercial interest," William Robbins discovered that

> tax-paid agriculture researchers worked on systems that [bred] vegetables for survival in mechanical har-vesters rather than for taste and food value . . . [and developed] hormones to promote livestock profits with no recorded advance research into attributes which might be harmful to health, as the notorious cancer-causing DES turned out to be.

As accusations, evaluations, and evasions escalated, eco-logical crisis intensified and economic and technological troubles increased criticism of and grassroots opposition to the skyrocketing costs of technocracy. It was the beginning of a broader recognition of the "sin of scientism," that fatal excess wherein methods of investigation used in the nat-ural sciences were applied to all fields of inquiry. Social at-titudes began to change on unexpected fronts. The United States Appeals Court for the District of Columbia, reject-ing the notion that "expert estimates of risk" should out-weigh public feeling, ruled in 1982 that the Nuclear Reg-ulatory Commission had to assess complaints of *psychological stress to the public* when determining the feasi-bility of activating another nuclear reactor at Three Mile Island, site of the 1979 Pennsylvania catastrophe. The same year, in Berkeley, California, 61 percent of the voters ap-proved an ordinance that banned the use of electroshock treatment for mental patients on the grounds that such treatment violated the constitutional right to privacy. Though later overturned by a state court, the ban was one

of many scattered signs of reaction against the presumption of scientific authority.

Crow wrote that further change would come, and believed that however much scientists might ignore mystery,
they were never immune to its force. He had discovered
that even Ivan Pavlov's faith in pure objectivity had wa-
vered toward the end of his life. Before Pavlov died

> he understood that his road had lengthened as he trav-
> eled it. . . . When [his] son Vsevolod lay dying of
> pancreatic cancer in 1935, Pavlov told him that per-
> haps the Communist state was making a mistake in
> trying to destroy the belief in an afterlife. "The com-
> mon people need the churches yet for a while. I must
> write a letter to Stalin," he said.

Of course I had to ask if this whole consideration should
not be put into perspective. How could science ever be divorced from modern lifestyle? But Crow replied that science could never accept responsibility for a holistic consideration of lifestyle

> because the circle of its mechanistic understanding has
> to be limited. Without *other* means—namely astrol-
> ogy or the I Ching—the scientist is not exploring but
> vainly trying to confine the cosmos to his own care-
> fully manicured farm. This is sad and sadder still when
> you consider that by doing so the scientist overlooks
> a valuable ancient premise that maintained that the
> hour a question is asked contains the answer. Unfor-
> tunately, like the futurist or the think-tank titan, the
> modern scientist is—in the end—actually nothing
> more than a corporate call boy. Corporations pay for

his tricks and pay the astronomical costs of his glittering barnyard, all the while reaping windfall profits from its produce.

The following day I wrote a long reply in which I detailed the work of psychologists, physicians, clergy, and scientists who were very aware of the extent to which their disciplines were divorced from mysticism. But it was seven months before I heard from Crow again, and then only by way of a motel postcard from Mansfield, Texas. On one side was a garish color photo of a curved cement driveway leading to the motel office, where a red cutout Eat sign leaned over an awning. On the other side he had written, "You need to look just a little bit longer and a little bit harder, old man. Someday you'll see, someday, when your winter is over."

Tell the boys and girls of the United States this world is theirs. If they have hearts of gold, a glorious new age awaits us. If they are honest, riches shall be theirs. If they are kind they shall save the whole world from malice and meanness. Will you take that message to the boys and girls of the United States, Jack Armstrong?
—*Jack Armstrong,* The All-American Boy

No matter what the season, I feared that Crow's dichotomy between science and lifestyle was extreme; nevertheless, it was crucial, and for greater consciousness to be pursued had to be understood. It was in lifestyle that the material applications of technology were translated into cultural consequences no individual could avoid, and translated into economic consequences of opportunity and income— so often the factor of final freedom—no democracy could ignore. But in modern America opportunity was too often an illusion and income too often an absurdity.

Writing in my journal on Friday, June 18, 1982, I noted that in the *San Francisco Chronicle,* a prized economist claimed

You had to make more than $2.6 million last year to rank among the top-paid executives in America. . . .
If you made one million dollars last year, you wouldn't even rank among top-paid executives.

Now it was the opinion of many that the *San Francisco Chronicle* was read in order to forget the world. That was unkind, but I could not help but notice that, in a year when lifestyle was threatened by unemployment and recession, a communications chair topped a list of successful executives by earning $22.5 million. He was followed by an executive whose product was toys, a link, of sorts, between technology and lifestyle . . . one that produced a paradox in which it was impossible to separate the figure of the executive from that of the scientist. Both were totems of a familiar economic pyramid that was used to illustrate the distribution of wealth, the rich on top, the poor below. It was an image that came to mind whenever I tried to decide if the technocracy that resulted from scientific materialism was guided by the ethics of science or the natural restraints which business claimed regulated its own conduct. Considering the threat of radioactive waste or the tragedy of unemployment, it was obvious the ethics of science were too remote or the restraints of business too lax, for there was a curious parallel between the claims of scientific detachment and the expediency of business. This expediency had been established in 1925 by Calvin Coolidge, the president who had proclaimed that the business of America was business, a haunting political quip that was eventually used to justify executive privilege.

Executive privilege had been crudely utilized by the great robber barons, who had amassed fortunes in the late 1800s. At the turn of the century, this utilization was checked by antitrust laws, but executive expediency and privilege soon developed more devious alternatives. When, in 1929, Alfred P. Sloan, Jr., long-time chief executive of General Motors, and a legend in American business, was urged to provide safety glass in General Motors automobiles, he was unimpressed by the fact that Ford had used safety glass for years. In secret correspondence he wrote that, accidents or no accidents,

> my concern in this problem is a matter of profit and loss. I may be all wrong but I feel that General Motors should not adopt safety glass for its cars and raise its prices. Our gain would be purely temporary.

Twenty-three years later a similar privilege was exercised by Charles E. Wilson, another chief executive of General Motors, who told a Senate committee that whatever was good for General Motors was good for America. This attitude provided the basis for the politically repeated insinuation that corporate well-being ultimately benefited the well-being of every American. To a limited degree this might have been true, but what was more important was the degree to which corporate well-being influenced national lifestyle and the consciousness of the individual. As early as 1974 the historian Richard J. Barnet worried that the shadow of corporate well-being had reached unwieldy proportions and was producing "a global reach," which demanded "in essence . . . the right to transcend the nation-state and, in the process, transform it."

Into what?

Detractors feared the global reach of corporations constituted an economic imperialism that created desire at the expense of necessity. Barnet told how

> in certain Peruvian villages a pathetic item is a piece of stone painted to look like a transistor radio. Peasants

too poor to buy the real one carry it for status . . . in a country . . . where, it is estimated, a substantial number of all babies born begin life with serious, and possibly irreparable, brain damage due to malnutrition.

To counteract criticism, expediency was made into a reason for privilege as well as a justification for the veneration of "the bottom line," the measurement of results solely in terms of profit and loss. Authority for this determination had been established for corporations long before World War II by an endless series of judicial rulings that established corporate independence from the nation-state and freed the executive from responsibility for such things as toxic shock or thousands of spent-fuel assemblies. Executives were legally responsible for little more than the profit of the corporation or the extent to which bottom lines were open to interpretation. Even with my limited view of the publishing industry, I had been able to observe enough to understand how easily bottom lines could be manipulated to reflect aims or revise conclusions that supported policy or decisions that might otherwise have appeared shortsighted, perhaps self-serving. The greater the investment, the more complex the bottom line, and the more ingenuity could be brought to bear on adjustment.

Until the Vietnam War it seemed that the conflict between individual welfare and corporate independence had been more or less contained, but after American government expenditure of billions of dollars on armaments and war materiel, the influence of American corporations on individual lifestyle grew to staggering proportions. Enriched by historic domestic consumption and the homogeneity of the international marketplace, corporations developed into conglomerates for which global investment began to have greater impact on corporate policy than national concerns. Mirow and Maurer traced the dynamics of this expansion back to international cartels that survived World War II. Studying webs of corporate power, they were able to explain how cartels not only survived but extended subtler methods of collusion and how American corporations

> led the initial wave of TNC (transnational corporations) expansion. In 1946 the total book value of U.S. direct foreign investment was $7.2 billion; by 1975 it had shot up to $137 billion.

Until 1980 individual income and small business opportunity paralleled corporate success in such a way that a global reach seemed acceptable, but after 1980, as small business opportunity began to suffer and personal bankruptcies rose to alarming levels (while corporate profits continued to rise) it was apparent something was dreadfully wrong. It was not difficult to conclude that the angle of the economic pyramid in America had been extensively sharpened. Translated into terms of individual lifestyle, this was not only depressing but proved that the growth of the global corporation had not been of benefit to the economic well-being of the majority of Americans . . . all of which contradicted the survival hymn of Republican politicians, who insisted that corporate health resulted in economic well-being that "trickled down" to other majorities.

The idea was patently false.

By 1982 America had slipped to tenth place in per capita gross national income, and with a rise in national debt fur-

ther decline was inevitable. These statistics were made
more bitter by the fact that air pollution in America exceeded that of every other industrial nation in the world.
Smoke from coal-burning utilities at Black Mesa in the
southwest corner of the United States had been photographed from Gemini space flights as early as 1964; at that
time Black Mesa pollution was the only industrial activity
visible from outer space. These realities offered the ines-
capable conclusion that the growth of corporate power had
led to a corporatization of American lifestyle. I remember
being repulsed and frightened by the idea: repulsed because
I resented this turn of events, and frightened because, short
of political nihilism, so little could be done about it.

Yet the warning signs were everywhere and often reflected in book projects submitted to the publishing association. An especially fascinating manuscript dealt with the
loss of individual freedom, a loss that inhibited awareness
and consciousness. It was an uneven but moving attempt
to show how potential for transformation of "the modern
everyperson" was being "slowly abased by a morass of political and material contradiction." Outlining how basic
needs of individual existence—shelter, food, transportation, and leisure—had been appropriated by complex corporate conspiracies that bordered on economic treason, the
author claimed individual transformation was being sacrificed for institutional prosperity. The argument was
based on the fact that throughout the country hundreds of
thousands of prosperous jobs—material means of transformation—had been eliminated when corporate planning
moved capital and manufacturing to foreign countries to
take advantage of cheap labor. In addition, government de-
regulation of industries had led to calculated reduction of

wages and benefits that were then used for further global diversification. Relaxation of banking regulations also encouraged questionable degrees of foreign expansion, and when the risk of relaxed regulation proved to be rash, failure was paid for by the American consumer or (in the case of bank failure) by the government, which then taxed the consumer. In addition to this, individual lifestyle suffered from the loss of single-family housing as well as from the mechanization of farming and food processing that had resulted in de facto corporate control of agriculture—the effects of which could be seen in any supermarket. In 1930 30 million people lived on farms and fed approximately 125 million Americans; fifty years later, 8 million people fed 210 million, "one of many trends that not only caused unemployment and cultural disorientation but furthered corporate influence over American lifestyle." The problem with the manuscript was that it offered few solutions.

During several editorial meetings the fate of "everyperson" was discussed at great length. Yet at the end of the table I began to wonder if it was time for me to begin to fade further from this trend of tirade. Schemes to expose science and attack corporations were as colorful as indictments in which executives became double-breasted carnivores who devoured power through conspiracies between business and science. And they were as informative as the explanation of how, historically, periods of scientific influence were distinguished by strong materialistic tendencies, and the theory that American materialism—with capitalism as a belief system—was being developed into a global totalitarianism. Orchestrated by executives, and enforced by legions of political partisans, lawyers, and militarists, this belief system allowed executive privilege to become a divine right and nurture a materialistic aristocracy that was served by consumers rather than vassals. But the fascination with all this faded when the discussions split into irreconcilable arguments, and all kinds of energy was wasted on blousey dialogues about socialized medicine, nationalization of utilities, guaranteed annual wage, and other radical strategies. Finally, one associate asked the overwhelming question: How relevant were collective concerns to the issues of the serious seeker? And did collective concerns leave room for the mystery without which the human condition withers?

That day there were no answers.

I tried to follow all of these considerations and for some months evaluate the growing social alienation felt by so many; but a second self always seemed to insist that these frustrations were produced by the very materialistic labyrinth I might well avoid. Besides, there were so many other ways to struggle. The fig leaf of the future was never fixed, and publishing was an effective weapon to wield against materialism, scientism, and all of the deception that threatened a positive change. There were always new fronts on which action could be taken. There was the absence of masculism, a long overdue exploration needed to complement the progress of feminism; the problem of the single vision in the novel; the dynamics of free will and volition. The advantages of meditation for the blind and handicapped had never been explored, and one of the most intriguing aspects of New Age potential came from diverse research that found a relationship between astrology and science. This speculation would hardly be accepted by traditional science, yet there had been a time when psychoneuroimmunology—the theory that the immune system could be psychologically enhanced—was hardly acceptable. As a matter of fact, many traditional scientists still dismissed in-depth analysis of "the four famous flaws" of Darwin, Freud, Einstein, and Bertrand Russell: Darwin's failure to see that natural selection did not apply to the human being; Freud's role in the disembodiment of the mind, the tragic ramifications of separating the body from the mind; Einstein's hesitancy to reconcile relativity with quantum physics; and Russell's distortion of mathematics through his implication that logic could explain the modern mathematical mystery.

I was satisfied there were endless ways to change, because there were always new ways to see, although years before, mindlessly motoring up and down the West Side Highway in New York, I never saw the extent to which the puritan ethic conflicted with change. Even if I had—with the top of the yellow convertible down and the radio playing—I would have seen it as a minor dichotomy. I needed to pass through the 1950s and the 1960s and the 1970s to see how the expediency of science and corporate power could be traced to executive privilege, and I needed to pass through the 1980s to see how the roots of such collusion reached into the highest office in the land. But I had too little awareness then. By the time such relationship became apparent, I could only recall that odd myopia of Herbert Hoover during the Great Depression—the purest example of privilege or expediency.

So I wrote to Crow, reviewing all of the presidents who had paraded through my life, but he only regretted that the list excluded Warren Harding, the handsome Hoosier who, "alongside John Kennedy, has to be remembered as one of the great romantics of American politics. As far as I'm concerned, Harding's cloakroom conquest of the teenaged Nan Britton was the pinnacle of political erotica that did more to humanize the pomp and circumstance of the White House than did the entire legacy of smiling First Ladies!"

Nevertheless, because the list was limited to my life, I had to exclude Harding.

As I reviewed presidential parades, I was pleasantly surprised by the degree to which they were dominated by Franklin D. Roosevelt . . . who was followed by seven others and Ronald Reagan. Yet, even overlooking personal prejudice, it became obvious how presidential privilege and expediency conflicted with puritan ethic. Harry Truman's presidency was plagued by a scandal of "five-per-centers" and a general, Harry Vaughn, whom Robert Ruark once remembered as having had "his hand so far in the national cash register that every time he saluted he waved the till." Oddly enough, along the routes, it was often impossible to tell whether privilege and expediency subverted the presidency or preserved it. Dwight Eisenhower left the office warning of the dangers of a military–industrial complex, yet many historians claimed it was formalized under his administration. That same complex tempted John Kennedy into the Bay of Pigs and led Lyndon Johnson into Vietnam; it fostered an expediency that ruined Richard Nixon, neutralized Gerald Ford, and doomed the idealism of Jimmy Carter. It also grew into an influence that compromised the difference between democratic standard and global opportunism.

Crow replied that such compromise was thousands of years old, but that was no consolation. A contaminated

American Dream was depressing . . . as depressing as the fact that, as presidential parades passed by, I stood in awe all the way.

Looking back, I realized it was innocent enthusiasm, for when I left Omaha as a boy and Greenwich Village as a young man, there were still grand dimensions to streets and highways. But the farther west I went the more uncertain they became. In the neighborhoods of George and Myra Babbitt, Willy and Linda Loman, and Walter and India Bridge, the presidency, magnified and moralized by media, seemed to turn into a featureless autocratic specter . . . as stern as Pluto and as oblivious to flattery, it loomed over glittering rows of attendant parvenus . . . an amazing mix of corporate callboys and generals turned defense contractors whose power prickled the crowds with awe.

Crow accused me of being a closet idealist, a posture that lent servitude to the materialistic aristocracy:

> You do not see! You still do not see that the presidency has become an insolently manufactured device! The American Dream has been media-ized into a candy coated, half-baked Orwellian cartoon in which opportunities become illusion and Big Brother nothing more than a great dyed head waving and posing beside a legacy of living lipstick.

*In the realm of human destiny, the depth of man's
questioning is more important than his answers.*
                                              —*Malraux*

I was in Los Angeles on business when Crow passed
through San Francisco for the last time, driving a dented
Chevrolet in which an expensive tape deck, wrapped in hotel towels, had been stuffed in the glove compartment.
Someone said he was traveling with an aloof young Mor-
mon divorcée from Salt Lake City and seemed to have
quite a bit of cash. That was odd, if not ominous. He had
discovered Sierra Pale Ale ("brewed in Chico—if you can
believe it!") and evidently spent long afternoons with cof-
feehouse regulars in North Beach discussing the art of removal, otherness, and his ongoing study of the "California
Impression," a phenomenon he claimed was a primary factor in American consciousness. He had stopped by my
place several times to pick up mail, leaving a $100 bill to
pay for an $87.77 COD package delivered the month be-
fore. It had come from an antique dealer in Becket, Mas-
sachusetts, and contained an original copy of the sheet music of a 1919 hit song, "Where Do Flies Go in the
Wintertime"—a typical addition to his collection of Amer-

icana still stored in an unused closet in a back room of my apartment.

The timing was regrettable. I would have given anything to have had the opportunity to spend a couple of days and nights finding out what he meant by the California Impression. More, I would have liked to discuss what I considered the failure of publishing to more effectively communicate consciousness to a wider audience. Months later I was forced to deal with these topics in expensive telephone conversations. One night we spent two hours analyzing the difference between a typical sale of twenty-five thousand copies of a consciousness title and a potential audience of twenty-five million people interested in modern psychology, medicine, religion, and science—or conduct, health, faith, and ecology. But Crow was optimistic. "I find those sales significant. You've got to remember that change is a dangerous product. Twenty-five million interested people probably have a duty to be prudent."

That was true enough.

"Then why be in a hurry? It's quite possible 25,000 readers can infect the thinking of the other 24,975,000. Slow up. Let go! These are tortuous times, and ideas—even exciting ones—have little immediate effect on loneliness, alienation, pollution, a two-trillion dollar national debt, or another war with Tripoli pirates. Remember, the only relief from fear is love, but those blinded by fear are in no condition to risk love. Sex? Yes—they'll risk sex. But love? Your American Emergency is that love is more dangerous than change! Weren't you the one who discovered that between 1955 and 1975 the divorce rate rose 250 percent? Think about the effect of that change on relationship. Be positive. Think about the changes in psychotherapy and

the investigation into scientific infallibility—about the revolution of the young—the sainthood of Martin Luther
King—women's rights—gay rights! How many of the 25
million interested people have truly assimilated all of that
and still have the courage or élan to look for love?"

I was not sure.

"And where would they look? In the traffic of Manhattan? In tantra triangles in Oakland or Laurel Canyon?
Never in Laurel Canyon. Cupid would never tolerate opi-
um suppositories. Oh no, love is never concerned with
sexual revolution. Love is the afterglow of spirituality. You
know what? The more I study romance in America, the
more I'm convinced that every relationship has to be
psychically assessed before sex begins. Otherwise desire
leads into the wrong arenas."

He sounded like a stoned moralist.

"No, not me! I've just discovered why the Gordian knot
of fidelity has been greased!" He liked that image and
laughed and told me to write it down.

I asked him what I would do with it.

"Hope that it might expose the difference between erot-
icism and love, and restore awareness of the need for romantic selectivity. Selectivity is the key to life. It not only
personifies awareness but reduces fear. What was that
quote from Rajneesh—that lovers know more than
saints—that lovers touch centers many yogis miss?"

I reminded him that Rajneesh had been deported!

"So? Wilhelm Reich ended up in jail! Only he didn't
have enough cash to buy his way out. His books were
burned by the United States government."

We had lengthier conversations about the California
Impression. At first I thought the California Impression

began in the 1950s, when Northern California became the testing ground for human potential, but that way was shortsighted. It seemed that the California Impression was a myth in that it did affect American ideology; at the same time it was a rudely shaped legend that influenced lifestyle and to understand it there was a need to understand the incongruous history of California.

Understanding began with the consideration that the original American Indians never migrated over the Bering Straits as anthropologists claimed; the red people originated in North America. Rather than ever crossing the Bering Straits from the north, they actually explored Canada and the Bering Straits from the south. These claims were being confirmed by the discovery of ancient sites in California and Arizona that predated anthropological claims. But the most important element of the incongruity was California's racial and cultural mix. The first migrants were Spanish explorers who came north from Central America and Russian traders who came south from Alaska. Both were followed in 1579 by Sir Francis Drake, who landed just above San Francisco Bay and claimed the territory for England. All of these claims were dissolved in waves of immigration that began two hundred years later when, lured by land, climate, and gold, pioneers completed the annihilation of the local Indians, who proved to be easy victims of the conquering Spanish.

In the 1800s the mix was further complicated by the importation of Chinese railroad workers and gradually redefined by white idealists and opportunists of every stripe—from ruthless railroad barons to the IWW Wobblie, Joe Hill, the first noble savage of American labor, and the ragworn Joads, fictionalized victims of the Great Depression. Formalized by the growing importance of San Francisco as a gateway to Asia and Los Angeles as a mecca for miracles, this serendipity was recognized in 1889 by Kipling, who felt a certain recklessness was in the West Coast air. He could not explain where it came from "but there it is. The roaring winds of the Pacific make you drunk to begin with."

Such intoxication was punctuated by the fact that in 1882 the population of California reached one million, and one hundred years later passed twenty-four million. Fed by natural resources and propelled by the flux of human energy, the results were provoked by political dissent and personified by social nonconformity. Contemporary prominence was assured by the growth of motion picture and television industries, although their ultimate products seldom contributed to human potential (their influence became more a commercial utility than a meaningful medium). Neither film nor television seemed able to profit from more subtle elements of the Impression, though others did.

Inspired by the climate and the geography, musicians, writers, artists, and poets were stirred by a special sympathy in which common restrictions of manners and mores were never completely established and an environment in which innovation was usually rewarded. The sympathy sustained Robert Louis Stevenson and Robinson Jeffers on the Monterey Peninsula; sheltered Nathaniel West, Thomas Mann, and Aldous Huxley in Los Angeles, and later supported Gary Snyder, Lawrence Ferlinghetti, and Richard Brautigan in San Francisco. Providing a peculiar license to profane, it encouraged human rights activism and resistance to the Vietnam War and, in the 1960s, caused artists and rock musicians to synthesize efforts in ways that had enormous political and cultural ramifications. Profiting from a rich revival of country music and a perennial appreciation of jazz—from the puritan fable as well as the oral ostracism of Beat poetry—the rock musician used music as social statement, and art complemented the integration. Utilizing but dramatically restyling aspects of modern art and the funk of Beat antiart, artists produced work that was not only gloriously conceived but, for all its experimental excess, was capable of exciting a wholesale demand for change. But as with other New Age extremes, the side effects often encouraged wantonness and reinforced a kind of pathfinder chauvinism that sometimes pervertedly groveled before media. These extremes frustrated critical examination and fostered a plastic hubris that could never be excused, even by the scenic sensuality of the Mojave Desert or the red-gold skeleton of the Golden Gate Bridge at twilight. Because of extremes, the California Impression had to be carefully evaluated.

Like the New Age, the California Impression had caustic critics. One sophisticated New York editor, unimpressed whenever he looked west, saw only a vision of "kindly elves at work among the eucalyptus trees," spinning little more than "threads and jewels of futurity." But that was an excessive determination that failed to recognize that lifestyle was as infected in Manhattan as in Marin County.

There is one story and one story only that will prove worth your telling.

—Robert Graves

Finally able to treasure the American experience and to better appreciate both sides of the country, I was satisfied with the cycle of change I had experienced, even if the mystery of consciousness had not been solved. Perhaps the complexity of consideration was too great. Whatever the reason, I could go on, older and wiser, with far fewer fears. I spent more time at home, reading and building additional bookshelves and sorting through publishing projects during the day and patterns of feeling at night.

I began to reorganize files and journals. Entries dating from the early 1950s, when I got out of the Army, were haphazard and incomplete, but by the time I left New York for California, the entries provided a continuous account of the countless moves and changes to and from places, and reflected an agelessness of people and events. In weird ways some entries had been transformed by time. Commentaries on being young and seemingly doomed by stifling conformity seemed fictionalized by time, and the very idea of revised lifestyle seemed to conflict with that rootlessness that Henry James recognized when he said that "being American was a complex fate."

I eventually combined some records and correspondence of the publishing association with other memorabilia—selected letters, photographs, newspaper clippings, articles and prudently unpublished poems, obituaries and reaction to various bedroom theater and world events—into an ambitious collage. I hoped to create some final perspective, but the material was too fragmented or rarefied.

I floundered for months before I realized that what repeatedly emerged from this effort was a growing acceptance of aging and death, a realization subject to all kinds of evasion. Nevertheless, it was the only level at which I could hope to see beyond all that I had come to believe and much I had come to fear. As in the past, I began to rely on meditation. Meditation provided an endless prairie on which I was able to shed final fears and face death openly rather than avoid it. To do this it became necessary to transform the negative concept of aging into the positive concept of longevity. The difference was dramatic. Emphasis on longevity revived belief in the power of aging and provided the mindfulness to anticipate death and to see through illusions of promise and prohibition that so tragically limited human potential. It was power that had been compromised by scientific certainty and discredited by simplistic geriatric attitudes that claimed it was sufficient to add years to life rather than life to years. In the light of contemporary demographics, the concerned individual was foolish not to sort out this confusion.

Well before the turn of the century the population in America had begun to show a steady increase in the number of old people. It was predicted that by the year 2000 one out of every four Americans would be older than sixty-five. Not only would the cultural and political character of society change, but its way of life would be dramatically affected by what Theodore Zeldin considered "the longing for gerontocracy." The most disturbing statistic was that in 1980 nearly one-third of every health care dollar was being spent on aging and the aged. Faced with an expected increase of old people, and the outrageous inflation of the cost of health care, it would be virtually impossible to continue such expenditure. There simply would not be enough public money.

The most impressive statistic was that by 1970 three thousand Americans had reached the age of one hundred; ten years later fourteen thousand had done so. Centenarians were the fastest growing minority, but their ranks were sadly imbalanced: there were nearly three women for every male. I wondered how many centenarians regularly exercised and fasted? How many were still sexually active, still attached to a family network of any kind, or were politically and culturally involved? How many were familiar with levels of awareness? How many studied other selves and began to seriously prepare for the last grand change? Demographics did not deal with those questions, or with an accepted sense of fatalism, especially about the fate of the body. John Tierney warned that as the American male reached middle age the skin lost moisture and the lenses of the eyes hardened. The body shrank and fattened, the shoulders narrowed, the nails grew more slowly, and stamina subsided. The head grew larger, the nose widened, and the mouth dried and gradually lost the acuteness of the sense of taste. What seemed most depressing was the degree to which reflexes slowed, testes sagged, and the angle of erection dipped below some official horizon.

Yeats, for whom old age was "a shipwreck," complained of the problem caused by "the devil" between his legs and wondered why old men should not be allowed to rail about the trials of time. In the spring of 1934, not content with poetic complaint, he acted and, according to Frank Touhy, "underwent the Steinach operation, a fashionable rejuvenation treatment through minor surgery intended to cause growth of the interstitial cells of the testicles." He was sixty-nine years old at the time, yet the operation gave him such energy that his remaining years proved to be fruitful and productive. In January of 1939 he died in France of pneumonia. Whether, as Auden wrote, "the death of the poet was kept from his poems," the death of the poet was not immediately announced to the public and only one bouquet arrived at the funeral. It had been sent by James Joyce.

Intrigued by this information, I discovered that Steinach died five years later, after a brilliant career in which his services had been sought by Freud, Jung, Charlie Chaplin, Leopold Stokowski, and even Pius XII, whom Crow always remembered as "the vampire pope" because of his refusal to speak out against the holocaust in the early 1940s. There seemed to be no conclusive evidence to prove how practical rejuvenation could be, and results were occasionally regrettable. In Europe in the 1920s a Russian physician, Serge Voronoff, implanted sliced monkey glands in the scrotums of hundreds of patients willing to pay up to $5000 for the procedure. This practice flourished until some patients unfortunately contracted syphilis from a monkey. Voronoff ultimately died in obscurity, but sounder alternatives eventually emerged. Royal jelly, derived from a substance produced by bees for the queen bee, and Gerovital, a procaine hydrochloride fortified with vitamin B, gained wide repute, yet I often wondered how Yeats's literary work would have been affected had his life been more holistically oriented and had he been freed of the anguish of traditional aging. If, at forty or fifty—better at thirty—he had begun to be concerned with psychophysiological well-being, as if it were part of a greater process, could he have worked onto still higher levels? But that was not the right question. The question was, How would I—without the vision of a Yeats—age and finally die?

One advantage that appreciated as time went on was warm and constant contact with my father, who was nearly eighty by the time considerations of longevity and death began to concern me. A soft-spoken, disappointed conservative who had been an electrical engineer, my father was dispassionate yet canny about aging, especially his own. He was seventy-nine when my mother died, stoned out of her mind by chemotherapy. After she passed away he steadfastly devoted himself to living alone and being independent, enjoying his children and grandchildren and remembering birthdays and holidays with long-distance telephone calls and a stream of carefully chosen, meticulously inscribed Hallmark greeting cards.

Whenever I was in New York on business, we still met for dinner, usually at the Clinton Inn in Tenafly, New Jersey, a place he had discovered shortly after our family moved east in 1945. By 1970 the restaurant had a decent wine list, so we could linger at the table while he patiently listened to my discourses on consciousness, unification, or the absence of the philosopher in the intellectual main-stream of America. He was only politely interested. Though I was encouraged to discuss exercise and diet, I was not encouraged to dwell on longevity or death. Sometimes, whenever I remembered to avoid those subjects, I looked at him across the table and wondered if we had ever passed each other in other roles in other lives. I knew he would have reacted as politely to the mention of past lives as he did to the quartets or schisms, but I also knew he would have ultimately shifted the conversation with the same precise determination with which he dismissed the sexual revolution or Watergate. As far as my father was concerned, Mick Jagger was merely today's Rudy Vallee and Richard Nixon and Ronald Reagan never were mentioned at dinner, if at all. After Watergate, discussions about politics or deficits, or any topic that related to the American Dream, were skillfully dodged.

I had no problem in getting him to discuss the past, but only within confines he had used in some thirty years of dinners at the Clinton Inn. It was easy to encourage him to explain why my grandfather was so misanthropic or to describe how my great-grandfather had migrated from Oswego, New York, to Omaha at the turn of the century. The recollections were repetitious but fascinating in that new facts or embellishments were usually added to the tales. During a few of these reviews, I would try to go within and visualize the 150 years that spanned our four lives and the slim succession of masculinity we represented. It would have been out of taste to hope the conversation could have touched on the psychic differences in our lives, or compare deaths. That would have jarred the tenor of dinner. The only thing I could do in that regard was innocently ask again what year it was my grandfather died and, when my father told me, try to *feel* the fact that I had had no contact whatsoever with my grandfather's last twenty years. We had "moved back East by then" and he was "back in Omaha," a senile old man of ninety in a nursing home a thousand miles away.

I revered the memory of my great-grandfather as much as I had resented the parsimony of my grandfather. At one of the last dinners in the Clinton Inn, my father revealed that my grandfather had inherited most of my great-grandfather's library, a collection of more than five thousand leather-bound volumes, yet admitted that "your grandfather terribly neglected that legacy." It seemed he surreptitiously sold the books whenever he needed money. It was galling to think that this must have been the fate of the Emerson essays I had lost in trade forty years before.

I never knew my great-grandfather. He died before I was born. In my files I had preserved his diploma from Oswego College, a picture of one of his Omaha houses, and one letter. The house was a generously porched and shaded three-story affair and, on the back of the picture, he had recorded that it had been built in 1884 and remodeled after a fire in 1903. The letter had been written to my father in 1918 when he was serving on the USS *Jenkins* off the Irish Coast during World War I. The handwriting was elegant and lovingly reported activities of my uncles and aunts and told of the wartime excitement in Omaha: "more parades, more marching of men in uniform and more of an expression of grim determination than there used to be." The tone was tinged with a kind of melancholy resignation which, when I was young, I so resented in old people. Not much had changed at home, a little though; Grandma and I are slowly going down the hill. . . . While you are just crossing the threshold at the entrance to manhood's prime, I am nearing the exit as the night comes on apace, waiting till the shadows have a little longer grown before I pass my life behind me.

Of course I demanded too much when I was young. In the 1950s I agreed with Dylan Thomas, who wanted the old to "rage against the dying of the light!" Yet after turning fifty, I realized such wrath would have been out of character for a man who graduated from Oswego College in 1862, migrated from New York to Nebraska, and could see he was nearing an exit where shadows had "a little longer grown."

I had resolved that conflict but could not overlook the fact that my great-grandfather, grandfather, and father lived their lives without going beyond the known, without asking why aging had to so diminish life—without attacking the silly supposition that youth was the prime of life when, in fact, it was little more than a confused struggle through the dreadful hypocrisy of material wastelands. None of them looked on death as the experience through which larger life might be realized. Years later I was content to modify the indictment. By then I could see how easy it was to become narcotized by the traditional acceptance of aging and die without striking out against the dreadful hypocrisy . . . without making some attempt, near the exit or in the shadows, to contact *and* experience "the great distinguished thing."

I did make one attempt to explore the shadows. In 1976, selecting two sensitive associates, I proposed a project tentatively titled *Hello Death!* The title was inspired by the desire for something rash, or pop, something that might cut through traditional folklore. The idea was to search out individuals who were near death or terminally ill, yet willing and able to be interviewed, individuals who would talk about their memories and visions, thoughts and feelings as they died. At our first editorial meeting we decided that each interview would be taped and that each subject would be photographed by a sensitive photographer. When someone else suggested the whole thing be filmed, there were strong objections. It was felt the hassle and technical demands of filmmaking would rupture spontaneous reaction and the media would exceed the event.

None of this was original. The process of the modern death experience had been well explored by Elisabeth Kübler-Ross, and there had been many attempts, both in books and films, to record death. A video artist, Jo Romans, filmed her own "creative suicide," and in 1974 a television newswoman, Chris Chubbuck, shot herself to death before a live camera in Sarasota, Florida, after announcing

> And now, in keeping with Channel 40's policy of always bringing you the latest in blood and guts in living color, you're about to see another first—an attempted suicide.

Yet it was hoped that *Hello Death!* might improve on all of this.

Whatever the method or medium, too few investigations had been directed at peaceful, orchestrated deaths, and those that had had been patchy and sentimental. Some were even dishonest and others nothing more than a melodramatic montage of the demise of some pooped or gnarled old person who was either pathetically unaware or balmy about the whole affair. Old Kodak snapshots were often blended with slick photography and punctuated with contrived narration or the selected comments of loved ones. An arty background of hometown streets and alleys was often used. At the end a symbolic white pigeon might be fluttered into space as the soundtrack squished out the rise of tinkling pianissimo. We decided against all that. We wanted pure reality controlled by the dying person who was aware. We wanted more life in death.

Nothing came of the *Hello Death!* project. One associate felt it unwise to try to reflect the potential of longevity through acceptance of the death experience, and the other concluded it would be meaningless to the young and ignored by the middle-aged, to whom death was more an unmentionable threat than a promise. The point was that the project would have no market until the recognition of longevity had replaced the idea of aging. I finally agreed that death was "impossible to sell in the stores." But these were not the only reasons the project was dropped. Vehement objections were raised whenever we searched for potential subjects. On one occasion, when we did find a terminal cancer patient willing to consider the project, we were threatened by relatives, and I was rudely admonished by a physician sitting inside of a Cadillac Seville, who thought the whole thing "a goddamned criminal intrusion!" Years later, organizing the journals, I happened on the *Hello Death!* file. By that time aging, longevity, and death were more salable subjects, but little inspiration rose out of the folder.

My father was eighty-six years old when he died. He knew he was near his exit and was resigned enough to finally refuse further cancer treatment, but it was obvious the disorientation of the coming experience was upsetting. Several times I flew back East to see him. The last trip was in the middle of a hot summer, so we would often retire to a lovely shaded patio of the convalescent hospital in order to enjoy the late afternoon. Of course he never mentioned the "great distinguished thing," but at one point he unexpectedly grasped my hand and held it for a long while. Finally, after looking away to study the shade, he thanked me for being a wonderful son and then, before I could react or reply, politely—but pointedly—asked what time my flight was leaving for San Francisco. I was not even scheduled to go that day, but was so overcome I mumbled something about seven o'clock in order that we both could agree I should be on my way. Though deeply moved, I knew he wanted to be alone. To honor that desire I left . . . turning only once to wave across the lawn from the parking lot. It was as if I saluted some strange absence of grief. As I did, it became apparent I might well live to become a centenarian in 2029.

One evening, several years later, as I stared across the living room and watched my wife chat and laugh softly on the telephone, I remembered that day, the last time I had seen my father. Only hours before, I had received news of the death of Mad Bear. When my wife's phone conversation ended, she rose, smiled, mentioned it was time for dinner, and left the room. I realized then that unless both of us were victims of some technological failure or natural disaster, one of us would die before the other. I recoiled from the realization, probably suffering from the same shock as those who once heard me ask if they knew of anyone who might agree to be interviewed as he or she died.

It was getting dark and, as I turned on the brass lamp, I wondered where I might be in 2029. Would I repeatedly take my daughter to the same restaurant? Would I have managed my last years with the same independence as my father? Would I avoid drugs and life-support systems in order to overcome disorientation, and experience, not suffer, my own end? Would I be able to see both sides of the line I crossed? To do that I knew I would have to sort hours as carefully as years in order to go beyond frontiers, real or imagined. Whatever the fate or the future, I felt a sudden exhilaration. If the change I had so long sought did not produce greater consciousness, it had begun a symmetry of understanding that made the world far richer.

Remembering it was Thursday, I paused. By the end of the week there would be another full moon, another chance to retreat, so there was little need to hurry. Life and death were the same trial.

End

REFERENCES

Preface
  p. xiv Rupert Brooke; from *The Great Lover*
Part I
  p. 3 Rilke; from *Malte Laurids Brigge*
  p. 13 Green; see *Beyond Biofeedback*, p. 219
  p. 14 Boyd; see *Rolling Thunder*, pp. 3, 5
  p. 14 Rolling Thunder; from taped transcription, Council Grove, Kansas, April 17, 1971
  p. 18 Lame Deer; see *Lame Deer Seeker of Visions*, p. 157
  p. 20 Henry Cogdall; see Edgar Lee Masters, from *The New Spoon River*
  p. 23 Roszak; see *Where the Wasteland Ends*, p. 277
  p. 30 Edwin Arlington Robinson
  p. 37 Jung; see *Psychological Reflections*, p. 285
  p. 42 emotional anatomy; see Keleman: *Emotional Anatomy*
  p. 51 Elizabeth Cady Stanton
  p. 53 Pelletier; see *Toward a Science of Consciousness*, p. 248

pp. 56–7 Young; see *The Reflexive Universe*, pp. 3, 5, 6, 7

p. 58 Smith; see *Forgotten Truth*, p. 30

p. 58 Roszak; see *Where the Wasteland Ends*, pp. 248, 252

Part II

p. 63 Yeats; see *Nineteen Hundred and Nineteen*

p. 68 Robert Oppenheimer; see *The Reflexive Universe*, p. 26

p. 68 Barbara Tuchman; see "The Historian's Opportunity," in *Saturday Review*, February 25, 1967

p. 69 Roszak; see *Where the Wasteland Ends*, p. 266

p. 70 Young; see *The Reflexive Universe*, p. 25

p. 73 Pelletier; see *Toward a Science of Consciousness*, p. 92

p. 73 Green; see *Beyond Biofeedback*, p. 184

p. 74 Jenkins; see *The Twenties*, p. 213

p. 74 Sir John Eccels; see Pelletier: *Toward a Science of Consciousness*, p. 68

p. 74 Paul Pietsch; see Pelletier: *Toward a Science of Consciousness*, p. 68; see also Pietsch, *Shufflebrain*

p. 76 Alice; from *Alice in Wonderland*

p. 78 cancer; see Peter Barry Chowka; *East West Journal*, March, 1981

p. 91 David Meltzer; see *Yesod*, p. 59

p. 93 Metzner; see *Maps of Consciousness*, p. 142

p. 94 Eastern master; see Timms: *Prophecies and Predictions*, p. 139

p. 99 Swami Vivekananda; see Wallbank: *Short History of India and Pakistan*, p. 101

p. 102 Peter Marin; see "Spiritual Obedience," in *Harper's*, February, 1979

p. 103 Sitwell; see *Noble Essences*, p. 4

p. 107 Saltoon; see *The Common Book of Consciousness*, p. 7

p. 107 Pelletier; see *Holistic Medicine*, p. 127

p. 109 Ballentine; see *Diet & Nutrition*, p. 313

p. 113 Hannah Arendt; see Rowes: *The Book of Quotes*, p. 235

p. 128 Kafka

p. 132 Grinspoon and Bakalar; see *Cocaine*, p. 21n

Part III

p. 141 Henry James; from *The Golden Bowl*

p. 144 Shapiro; see *Radwaste*, p. 44

pp. 145–6 Eiseley; see *The Man Who Saw Through Time*, pp. 17, 18

p. 147 Robbins; see *The Great American Food Scandal*, p. 174

p. 148 Pavlov; see *Makers of Modern Thought*, p. 291

p. 150 Jack Armstrong; from *Jack Armstrong, The All-American Boy*, circa 1949

p. 152 Alfred P. Sloan, Jr.; see Mintz and Cohen: *Power, Inc.*, p. 110

p. 152 Barnet and Muller; see *Global Reach*, pp. 15, 177

p. 154 Mirow and Mauer; see *Webs of Power*, p. 34

p. 161 Malraux; see Rowes: *The Book of Quotes*, p. 116

p. 167 Graves; from *To Juan at the Winter Solstice*

p. 169 Pelletier; see *Longevity*, p. 47

p. 169 Tierney; from "The Aging Body," in *Esquire*, May, 1986

p. 170 Touhy; see *Yeats*, p. 274

p. 170 Auden; from *In Memory of W. B. Yeats*

BIBLIOGRAPHY

Ballentine, Rudolph. *Diet and Nutrition: A Holistic Approach*. Honesdale, Pa.: Himalayan International Institute, 1978.

Barnet, Richard J., and Ronald E. Muller. *Global Reach: The Power of the Multinational Corporations*. New York: Simon & Schuster, 1974.

Bateson, Gregory. *Steps to an Ecology of Mind*. New York: Ballantine Books, 1972.

Bettelheim, Bruno. *Freud and Man's Soul*. New York: Alfred Knopf, 1982.

Boyd, Doug. *Rolling Thunder*. New York: Random House, 1974.

Butler, Kate. "Events Are the Teacher: Working Through the Crisis at the San Francisco Zen Center." *CoEvolution Quarterly*, Winter 1983.

Campbell, Joseph. *The Masks of God: Creative Mythology*. New York: Viking Press, 1968.

Capra, Fritjof. *The Tao of Physics*. Berkeley: Shambhala, 1975.

Castenada, Carlos. *The Teachings of Don Juan*. New York: Simon & Schuster, 1968.

de Beauvoir, Simone. *The Coming of Age*. New York: G. P. Putnam, 1972.

de Ropp, Robert S. *Warrior's Way*. New York: Delacorte Press/Seymour Lawrence, 1979.

Dufty, William. *Sugar Blues*. Radnor, Pa.: Chilton, 1975.

Dunlap, Caroll. *California People*. Salt Lake City: Peregrine Smith, 1982.

Edel, Leon. *Henry James: A Life*. New York: Harper & Row, 1985.

Eiseley, Loren. *The Man Who Saw Through Time*. New York: Scribners, 1961.

Goleman, Daniel. *The Varieties of the Meditative Experience*. New York: Dutton, 1977.

Goodman, Jeffrey, Ph.D. *American Genesis*. New York: Summit Books, 1977.

Green, Elmer, and Alyce Green. *Beyond Biofeedback*. Boston: Delacorte, 1977.

Grinspoon, Lester, and James B. Bakalar. *Cocaine: A Drug and Its Social Evolution*. New York: Basic Books, 1976.

Haich, Elizabeth. *Initiation*. Palo Alto, Calif.: Seed Center, 1960.

Huxley, Aldous. *The Doors of Perception*. New York: Harper & Row, 1954.

Jack, Alex. *The New Age Dictionary*. Brookline, Mass.: Kanthaka Press, 1976.

Jackson, Mildred, and Terri Teague. *The Handbook of Al-

ternatives to Chemical Medicine. Oakland, Calif.: Lawton-Teague Publications, 1975.

Jaynes, Julian. *The Origin of Consciousness in the Bicameral Mind*. Boston: Houghton Mifflin, 1976.

Jenkins, Alan. *The Twenties*. London: Peerage Books, 1974.

Jung, C. G. *Psychological Reflections*. New York: Harper & Row, 1953.

Kapleau, P. *Three Pillars of Zen*. Boston: Beacon Press, 1967.

Keleman, Stanley. *Living Your Dying*. New York: Random House/Bookworks, 1974.

———. *In Defense of Heterosexuality*. Berkeley: Center Press, 1982.

———. *Emotional Anatomy*. Berkeley: Center Press, 1985.

Koestler, A. *The Ghost in the Machine*. New York: Macmillan, 1968.

Krishna, Gopi. *The Awakening of Kundalini*. New York: Dutton, 1975.

Lame Deer, John (Fire), and Richard Erdoes. *Lame Deer, Seeker of Visions: The Life of a Sioux Medicine Man*. New York: Simon & Schuster, 1979.

Lausch, Christopher. *The Culture of Narcissism*. New York: W. W. Norton.

Leonard, George. *The Silent Pulse*. New York: Dutton, 1978.

Le Shan, Lawrence. *How To Meditate*. New York: Bantam, 1975.

Macbeth, Norman. *Darwinism: A Time for Funerals*. San Francisco: Robert Briggs Associates, 1985.

Magaziner, Ira C., and Robert B. Reich. *Minding American Business*. New York: Harcourt, Brace, 1982.

Mails, Thomas E. *Fools Crow*. New York: Doubleday & Co., 1979.

Makers of Modern Thought. New York: American Heritage Publishing, 1972.

Mann, W. Edward, and Edward Hoffman. *The Man Who Dreamed of Tomorrow*. Los Angeles: J. P. Tarcher, 1980.

Marin, Peter. *Spiritual Obedience*. New York: *Harper's Magazine*. February, 1979.

Masters, Edgar Lee. *The New Spoon River*. New York: Macmillan, 1968.

Masters, R. E., and J. Houston. *Varieties of Psychedelic Experience*. New York: Holt, Rinehart & Winston, 1966.

McKenna, Terrence. *The Invisible Landscape—Mind, Hallucinogens and the I Ching*. New York: Seabury Press.

Meltzer, David. *Yesod*. London: Trigram Press, 1969.

Metzner, Ralph. *Maps of Consciousness*. Collier Books: New York, 1971.

Mendelsohn, Robert S. *Male Practice—How Doctors Manipulate Women*. Chicago: Contemporary Books, 1982.

Miller, Roberta DeLong. *Psychic Massage*. New York: Harper & Row, 1975.

Mintz, Morton. *By Prescription Only* (originally published as *The Therapeutic Nightmare*). Boston: Beacon Press, 1967.

Mintz, Morton, and Jerry S. Cohen. *America, Inc.: Who Owns and Operates the United States*. New York: Dial Press, 1971.

———. *Power, Inc.: Public and Private Rulers and How To Make Them Accountable*. New York: Viking Press, 1976.

Mirow, Kurt Rudolph, and Harry Mauer. *Webs of Power: International Cartels and the World Economy*. Boston: Houghton Mifflin, 1982.

Mishlove, Jeffrey. *The Roots of Consciousness*. New York: Random House/Bookworks, 1975.

Monroe, Robert. *Journeys of the Body*. Garden City, N.Y.: Doubleday & Co., 1971.

Muktananda. *Selected Essays*. Edited by Paul Zweig. New York: Harper & Row, 1976.

Needleman, Jacob. *Sin and Scientism*. San Francisco: Robert Briggs Associates, 1985.

Neihardt, John G. *Black Elk Speaks*. New York: William Morrow, 1932.

Ornstein, Robert E., ed. *The Nature of Human Consciousness*. San Francisco: W. H. Freeman, 1973.

Palmer, Cynthia, and Michael Horowitz. *Shaman Woman, Mainline Lady: Women's Writings on the Drug Experience*. New York: Quill Books (William Morrow), 1982.

Pearce, Joseph Chilton. *Exploring the Crack in the Cosmic Egg*. New York: The Julian Press, 1974.

Pelletier, Kenneth R. *Mind as Healer, Mind as Slayer: A Holistic Approach to Preventing Stress Disorders*. New York: Dell, 1977.

———. *Holistic Medicine: From Stress to Optimum Health*. New York: Dell, 1979.

———. *Longevity: Fulfilling Our Biological Potential*. New York: Delta Books, 1981.

———. *Toward a Science of Consciousness*. Berkeley: Celestial Arts, 1985.

Penfield, Wilder. *The Mystery of the Mind*. Princeton, N.J.: Princeton University Press, 1976.

Pietsch, Paul. *Shufflebrain*. Boston: Houghton Mifflin, 1981.

Rajneesh, Bhagwan Shree. *The Book of Secrets*. New York: Harper & Row, 1974.

Robbins, William. *The Great American Food Scandal*. New York: William Morrow & Co., 1974.

Rodarmor, William. "The Secret Life of Muktananda." *CoEvolution Quarterly*, Winter 1983.

Roszak, Theodore. *Where the Wasteland Ends*. New York: Doubleday & Co., 1972.

————. *Person/Planet*. Garden City, N.Y.: Doubleday & Co., 1979.

————. *The Cult of Information*. New York: Pantheon, 1986.

Rowes, Barbara. *The Book of Quotes*. New York: Ballantine Books, 1979.

Saltoon, Diana. *The Common Book of Consciousness*. San Francisco: Chronicle Books, 1979.

Schroeder, Eric. *Zodiac: An Analysis of Symbolic Degrees*. San Francisco: Robert Briggs Associates, 1982.

Schumacher, E. F. *Good Work*. New York: Harper & Row, 1979.

Schwarz, Jack. *Voluntary Controls*. New York: Dutton, 1978.

————. *Human Energy Systems*. New York: Dutton, 1979.

Shadowitz, Albert, and Peter Walsh. *The Dark Side of Knowledge*. Reading, Mass.: Addison-Wesley, 1976.

Shah, Indries. *The Sufis*. New York: Doubleday, 1964.

Shapiro, Fred. *Radwaste*. New York: Random House, 1982.

Sheldrake, Rupert. *A New Science of Life: The Hypothesis of Formative Causation.* Los Angeles: J. P. Tarcher, 1983.

Silverman, Milton, Philip R. Lee, and Mia Lydecker. *Prescriptions for Death: The Drugging of the Third World.* Berkeley: University of California Press, 1982.

Sitwell, Osbert. *Noble Essences.* New York: Grosset & Dunlap, 1950.

Skinner, B. F. *Beyond Freedom and Dignity.* New York: Knopf, 1971.

Smith, Huston. *Forgotten Truth: The Primordial Tradition.* New York: Harper & Row, 1976.

Suzuki, D. T. *The Field of Zen.* London: The Buddhist Society, 1969.

Szasz, Thomas. *The Myth of Mental Illness.* New York: Harper & Row, 1974.

————. *Schizophrenia: The Sacred Symbol of Psychiatry.* New York: Basic Books, 1976.

Teilhard de Chardin, P. *The Phenomenon of Man.* Translated by B. Wall. New York: Harper Torchbooks, 1961.

Temple, Robert K. G. *The Sirius Mystery.* London: Sidgwick & Jackson, 1976.

Timms, Moria. *Prophecies and Predictions.* Santa Cruz, Calif.: Unity Press, 1980.

Touhy, Frank. *Yeats.* New York: Macmillan, 1976.

Wallbank, T. Walter. *A Short History of India and Pakistan from Ancient Times to the Present.* New York: Mentor Books, 1958.

Waters, Frank. *Book of the Hopi.* New York: Ballantine Books, 1963.

Watkins, T. H. *California: An Illustrated History.* New York: American Legacy Press, 1983.

Watts, Alan. *Beat Zen Square Zen and Zen*. San Francisco: City Lights Books, 1959.

Weil, Andrew. *The Natural Mind: A New Way of Looking at Drugs and the Higher Consciousness*. Boston: Houghton Mifflin, 1972.

Weiner, Michael, and Kathleen Goss. *The Complete Book of Homeopathy*. New York: Bantam Books, 1982.

Wheelis, Allen. *The End of the Modern Era*. New York: Basic Books, 1971.

White, Lynn, Jr. *Machina Ex Deo: Essays in the Dynamism of Western Culture*. Cambridge, Mass.: M.I.T. Press, 1968.

Wilson, Colin. *The Outsider*. Boston: Houghton Mifflin, 1956.

————. *Mysteries*. New York: G. P. Putnam & Sons, 1979.

Wittner, Lawrence S. *Cold War America From Hiroshima To Watergate*. New York: Praeger Publishers, 1974.

Young, Arthur M. *The Bell Notes: A Journey from Physics to Metaphysics*. San Francisco: Robert Briggs Associates, 1984.

————. *The Reflexive Universe*. San Francisco: Robert Briggs Associates, 1985.

INDEX